Praise for *The Idea Generator*

❚❚ Insightful and practical, this book will provide you with fantastic advice on how to generate better ideas in your business.

ODED RAN, CHIEF EXECUTIVE OFFICER, TOUCHNOTE

❚❚ Chris challenges traditional approaches on how creative new ideas are generated, and provides valuable alternative tools to use on a daily basis to make innovation happen.

BILL JARRARD, CO-FOUNDER, MINDWERX INTERNATIONAL

❚❚ *The Idea Generator* is not just a set of tools but a way of thinking to help design tomorrow in a practical, easy to digest way.

ROB MILLAR, MANAGING DIRECTOR, COMOTION CONSULTING LTD

❚❚ Trigger the innovative side of your brain with the most comprehensive and powerful guide on the market.

ALEJANDRO MAROTO, HEAD OF INNOVATION AND NEW BUSINESS SERVICES, TELEFÓNICA BUSINESS SOLUTIONS

❚❚ For a new and pragmatic approach to business growth, *The Idea Generator* is the book you need.

STEVE WESTON, FORMER CEO OF MORTGAGES, BARCLAYS BANK

❚❚ Powerful, no-nonsense, business thinking tools.

STUART MITCHELL, GROUP CEO, SIG PLC

▐▐ Chris Thomason shows you how to ask 'killer questions' and produce game-changing ideas. *The Idea Generator* is smart, original, and highly useful.

WARREN BERGER, BEST-SELLING AUTHOR, *A MORE BEAUTIFUL QUESTION*

▐▐ Chris Thomason is one of the most creative and innovative thinkers I know – he is always coming up with new ideas and sharing those with me to help my company. He has even taken it so far as to package his idea so I can literally visualize what the end product might look like.

His initiative and passion for bringing new ideas to life is what has gone into his book, *The Idea Generator*. I believe all of us can use a boost once in a while to finding ways to be more creative in what we do each day.

Chris lays out a simple approach that is easy to follow and implement – no matter who you are. Enjoy Chris's personality throughout . . . he is one in a million.

KERRI K. NELSON, CEO AND PRESIDENT, CUSTOMERSFIRST NOW

The Idea
Generator

PEARSON

At Pearson, we believe in learning – all kinds of learning for all kinds of people. Whether it's at home, in the classroom or in the workplace, learning is the key to improving our life chances.

That's why we're working with leading authors to bring you the latest thinking and best practices, so you can get better at the things that are important to you. You can learn on the page or on the move, and with content that's always crafted to help you understand quickly and apply what you've learned.

If you want to upgrade your personal skills or accelerate your career, become a more effective leader or more powerful communicator, discover new opportunities or simply find more inspiration, we can help you make progress in your work and life.

Every day our work helps learning flourish, and wherever learning flourishes, so do people.

To learn more, please visit us at **www.pearson.com/uk**

The Idea Generator

15 clever thinking tools to
create winning ideas quickly

Chris Thomason

PEARSON

Harlow, England • London • New York • Boston • San Francisco • Toronto • Sydney
Auckland • Singapore • Hong Kong • Tokyo • Seoul • Taipei • New Delhi
Cape Town • São Paulo • Mexico City • Madrid • Amsterdam • Munich • Paris • Milan

Pearson Education Limited
Edinburgh Gate
Harlow CM20 2JE
United Kingdom
Tel: +44 (0)1279 623623
Web: www.pearson.com/uk

First edition published 2016 (print and electronic)

ISBN: 978-1-292-15601-9 (print)
      978-1-292-15602-6 (PDF)
      978-1-292-15603-3 (ePub)

British Library Cataloguing-in-Publication Data
A catalogue record for the print edition is available from the British Library

Library of Congress Cataloging-in-Publication Data
A catalog record for the print edition is available from the Library of Congress

10 9 8 7 6 5 4 3 2 1

20 19 18 17 16

Cover design by Two Associates
Front cover image © istock

Print edition typeset in 10.25pt Frutiger by Aptara
Printed by Ashford Colour Press Ltd, Gosport

NOTE THAT ANY PAGE CROSS REFERENCES REFER TO THE PRINT EDITION

For James and Stephanie

May all your dreams become ideas and may all your ideas become reality

Contents

About the author

Chris Thomason is a Chartered Engineer and a Fellow of the Institution of Mechanical Engineers. He started his career in the UK automotive industry before emigrating to South Africa to work in the gold and platinum mining industry, where he was fortunate to experience the transition to democracy at first hand. He also spent time running a gold mine in Mozambique at the height of the civil war.

Chris moved to Australia in 1999 to work in the field of business innovation in such diverse areas as helping an insurance company create £46 million in new revenues from two minor product changes; helping Canon identify the future of imaging 25 years out; and shaping the development of the Sydney 2000 Olympics site after the games.

Having returned to the UK and worked with organisations to develop new services and customer experiences, Chris founded Ingenious Growth to develop one of his passions: the application of better thinking to key issues in business and society.

Acknowledgements

Profound thanks are owed to Eloise Cook at Pearson Education, who supported a myriad of questions from me during the writing of *The Idea Generator*. Also to Moira Wills of the Reigate School of Art at East Surrey College who introduced me to artist Issy Ana Porcel and illustrator Sam Barker, two extremely talented individuals who provided the illustrations in the book. My colleague Steve Heron also gave valuable input into thinking about things differently.

Publisher's acknowledgements

Illustrations on pages 3, 9, 25, 37, 49, 55, 91, 121, 155 and 167 by Issy Porcel. Illustrations on 56, 60, 61, 62, 63, 67, 69, 70, 75, 81, 84, 93, 99, 105, 108, 112, 117, 123, 128, 135, 140, 146 and 151 by Sam Barker. All other illustrations are the author's own.

Getting your mind around an issue

There are two types of people in the world.

Those who classify people into two groups and those who don't.

While this may appear to be simply a humorous statement, it carries a remarkable degree of insight about thinking. For there are two types of people involved in the pursuit of new ideas that will deliver an amazing outcome for them. There are those people who are highly motivated and passionate in their approach to identifying a new idea that represents a great opportunity for them – and there are those who aren't.

This doesn't imply that those individuals who aren't actively involved in pursuing a new idea don't want one – it's just that they aren't doing anything about it. They are passively hoping that a great idea will occur to them in a moment of good fortune or serendipity. Well it might. And they might win the jackpot on the lottery too, for the odds are probably about the same.

Whichever type of person you are, this book is written to help you. For those of you who are actively involved in creative thinking around any subject, *The Idea Generator* will provide a range of tools and approaches that will help you – no matter what stage of development your idea is at. And for those of you who aren't formally applying your thinking abilities – it provides you with a structured approach that will accelerate you from a standing start to becoming successfully engaged in your search for your own idea in a remarkably short space of time.

An idea can change the world

This may sound like a cliché from a 1990s motivational poster (that invariably showed an athletic-looking person staring over a landscape from a mountain top), it's actually the truth on which all businesses are founded. Way back in time, at the starting point on the timeline of every successful business, someone posed a different or unusual question – and then answered it with a new idea. This idea undoubtedly spawned more ideas, which coalesced into an enticing proposition which formed the basis of its success.

Whether it's a business idea that actually changes the world, such as Facebook changing the way that a huge chunk of the world's population interacts, or if it boosts your business in some way or benefits your family life – then it's improving your personal world. As long as it's to your benefit, it can be seen as a success – regardless of the scale of that success.

But how is your world potentially being changed by others? Consider the fact that at this very moment in time:

- There's a middle-manager toying with an idea that, when launched, will make them a star in your business due to the success it will deliver.
- Someone with less experience than you is working on a new start-up that will be worth over £20 million to them in five years' time.
- A competitor in your industry is working on an idea that will help their business to make dramatically more profits – potentially at the expense of your business.

People are working on business ideas right now. Some that will benefit your business, and some that have the potential to harm your business. However, the process of identifying new business opportunities is much the same regardless of scale. Whether you're a corporate looking for a £25 million opportunity, a mid-sized company looking for a £2.5 million opportunity, a small business looking for a £250,000 opportunity – or even an individual looking to find a new way around an old problem, the creative, mental effort required for success, bizarrely, is quite similar. These are all success levels that are achievable (and have been achieved and surpassed) by The Idea Generator process. They represent targets that are readily attainable for you as long as you have the ability and the thinking mechanisms to deliver them. Later, you can start to think bigger – but for now, this is probably a more-than-adequate benefit from a thinking process that is new to you.

Your idea can change your world

For the two types of people with their different approaches to thinking mentioned at the start, the ones who are busy on an idea are already heads-down and occupied with their creative activities. However, for those of you not actively pursuing an amazing new idea of your own – then you may want to ask yourself why you aren't doing something. Because right now, at this very moment, there's an idea you could have that would offer up a tremendous opportunity that could change your world. But you're never going to find it if you don't open your mind to looking for it.

And it isn't just about world-changing business activities either, for as you read this sentence:

- A young teenager is designing an item of clothing which they don't yet realise will form the start of their career as a top fashion designer.
- Someone is authoring their first novel that will win them a major book prize.
- A middle-aged woman who is wondering what she should do now her children have left home is watching a TED talk on YouTube that will become her new passion for the rest of her life.
- A person similar to you is preparing for a meeting with a potential employer where they will propose an 'edgy' idea that will change their life in amazing ways.

It doesn't matter who you are, what you are, or where you are, you are capable of asking a question – and that's all it takes to get started. And when you get a great idea that's a relevant and practical answer to your question, then you have an automatic edge over almost everyone else. You have the proven ability to pose and creatively answer valuable questions. It's this edge that can help you to repeatedly think your way to more creative successes.

While this book is heavily focused on finding practical and valuable winning ideas for the business environment, it's individual employees who do the thinking. This is why *The Idea Generator* tools are appropriate not just for large companies and organisations, but for smaller businesses and individuals outside of the business environment too. It takes much the same amount of effort, thinking activity and brainpower to develop an amazing new idea for yourself as it does for your business. So why not practise on personal issues too?

Have you got an issue that a single powerful idea could make disappear or convert the current situation into a massive opportunity for you? The answer to this is almost certainly 'yes' – and many times over – because there are countless issues you could address and countless ways to address each one of them.

So you have a choice. Either you can accept your situation and live with it, and try to work your way out, around or through it in the usual manner with the usual results – or you can make something different happen. You can have a new idea. But you aren't going to get a new idea unless you actively start looking for one. As the UK national lottery slogan says, 'Play makes it possible'. You can't win unless you decide to play, and the more you play the greater your chance of winning. Unfortunately, with the lottery the only way you can increase your chance of winning is through luck in picking the correct numbers and improving your odds by buying lots of tickets. There's little skill involved at all.

However, with ideas, it's all about skill. And you can improve your chance of winning by using some clever thinking tools. Wouldn't being able to pick your six winning numbers be a lot easier if you could do it after three numbers had already been drawn? With clever thinking you can effectively make this happen for the issue you want to consider.

What's this book going to do for you?

Rather than creative thinking being considered a fluffy and serendipitous affair, *The Idea Generator* will show you how to use focused and applied thinking to achieve the results you desire. There are three toolsets that will help you apply an alternative, rigorous and progressive approach to your business and personal thinking. Each process is targeted to deliver results in distinctly different areas. The three areas are:

1 Finding pragmatic, fresh ideas on a new project
2 Overcoming an old and problematic issue
3 Identifying organic, business-growth opportunities

The purpose of the book is to offer some proven techniques and to provide a templated approach to guide you effectively through their use. There aren't any long justifications and case studies, just processes that with hindsight will appear to be common sense, and that are worth giving a go. And that's the aim – for you to give it a go.

This isn't a book to read to pass the time. It's a workbook that helps you achieve success by guiding you through the thinking templates that you can download from The Idea Generator website. It's written as a punchy and practical 'how to' guide with content that focuses on the application of the tools for delivering big thinking for winning business ideas. The templates are free to download and you can use them to work through your thinking projects. The use of the three templates is clearly demonstrated in the following chapters, so you may wish to download and print them out now – and to keep them handy as you read the book. You'll be using them when you do your first thinking project. The templates can be found at **www.TheIdeaGenerator.info**

Why today's thinking is so outdated

Stock markets tumble

Unions grumble

Pensions investment fumble

Will the EU crumble?

Banner headlines love using the negative-sounding '-umble' words. Yet while these may be just headlines, they are succinct pointers to the big issues that big business faces today. But this isn't a new thing, for big business has always faced big issues – and always will. To handle these big issues they recruit smart, skilled people and put processes and systems in place to support them. Unfortunately, this isn't guaranteed to help these smart, skilled people to resolve all the big issues they come up against. Especially the ones that are in need of a new and creative business solution.

Being paid to know the answers isn't always a good thing

If you're employed by a business and are reading this book, the chances are you're smart and talented. You must have a level of knowledge and expertise in some area that your employer values – which is why they offered you a job in the first place. Unfortunately, it's this knowledge and expertise that may be stopping you from being inno-vative. Why? Because as an expert you are generally expected to know the answers to any questions that arise in your business that relate to your domain of skill and knowledge.

As an example, imagine you went to your superior with a big and bold question that you had no idea how to answer. Which of these three responses are you most likely to receive?

1 Don't bring me problems, bring me solutions.

2 You're expected to know the answer to this – it's what we pay you for!

3 I thought this was your area of expertise?

Hardly the sort of response that stimulates the asking of new and intriguing questions in your area, is it?

An alternative approach that you can test out is the next time a senior manager asks you a question, try answering it with 'I don't know' or 'Sorry, I haven't got a clue' or 'I'll need to spend some time finding a new answer to that'. Responses like this are likely to be serious CLMs (Career Limiting Moves), for there's a corporate expectation that every-thing should be known.

The educationalist and creative expert Sir Ken Robinson summed this up by saying, 'In our culture, not to know is to be at fault, socially.' You, as an expert in your field, always need to be seen to know the answers – but in doing so you tend to repeat, recycle and upcycle things that you've done before, and that you know will work. Because that's what experts do.

Frequently, this is acceptable – for when an existing and known solu-tion will work satisfactorily, then there's no need to expend further effort on the issue. But when do you make the judgement call that it's time to review the situation from anew and do something different? The easier route is always the known over the unknown.

We shield ourselves from exploration

We inherently love answering questions that only we know the answers to, as this cements our place in the organisation as the expert in a given field. And it also fuels our self-esteem. However, to be innovative we have to do something new – and that's to go beyond the realms of our existing knowledge and to find some new things. *Some things that are unknown.* And this is worrisome for an expert because it's intended to highlight the things that we don't know.

When Captain James Cook was on his voyage of discovery (1768–1771), it included his search for the hypothetical Terra Australis – the presumed great southern continent. From the top mast of Cook's ship, HMS *Endeavour*, a crew member could only see a distance of 12 miles in any direction to the horizon due to the curvature of the Earth. They couldn't be sure where to go, so they went where they saw birds flying, or where they saw fresh foliage in the sea – and of course where the prevailing winds took them. They had to follow these hunches as they had such a limited view in the vastness of the Pacific Ocean.

This is true exploration. And in true explorer style, they traversed an erratic course, but on their journey they made amazing discoveries – such as New Zealand and Australia. The botanists in the crew also discovered many smaller things, such as new species of plants and animals. The diagram below shows the route that Cook may have taken in his exploration.

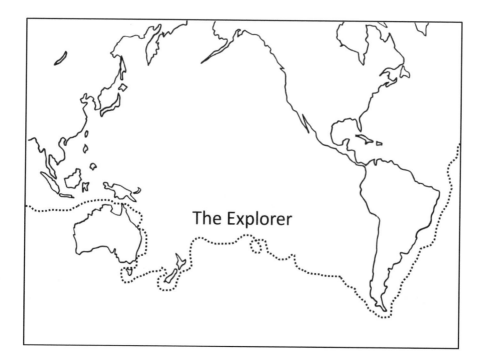

The Explorer

When you are on an international journey by plane and resort to reading the in-flight magazine, invariably towards the back will be a map of the routes that the airline flies. These will be depicted as straight lines traversing the globe from central hubs like London, Dusseldorf or New York and covering all major points on the planet. This representation is analogous to how an expert thinks. They like to go directly from a question to an answer. If Captain Cook had been an expert rather than an explorer, then his journey may have potentially been more like this:

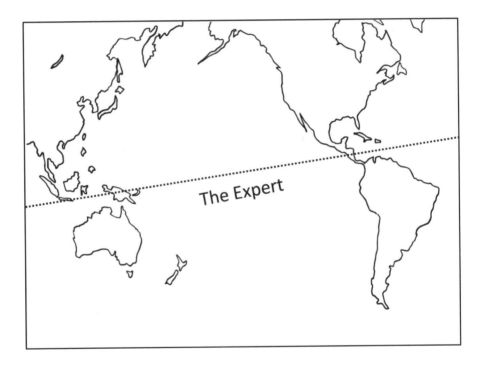

He'd have completed his journey much quicker but would have missed out on discoveries like New Zealand and Australia. For innovation to happen, where new things are discovered, we have to be willing to meander and explore – but frequently this isn't in the nature of an expert.

To start out on a journey to discover new answers and opportunities, we've got to prepare to get at least a little bit lost – and to start out by asking a question to which we don't have any immediate answers.

We need to be asking big and bold questions. But before we can do this, first we need to understand why we are fearful of asking powerful questions of this nature.

Why our expertise fears difficult questions

If, as a business, you ask yourself the question, 'Where will we get an additional five per cent increase in revenues this year?', the solution isn't likely to be some radical change to your business, or some game-changing new product. It's likely to come from a series of smaller changes that will each add value and which accumulate to give the desired additional five per cent result. These smaller changes will most likely appear to be blindingly obvious in hindsight – as all the best new ideas are. Unfortunately, this can have the potential to make the expert look a little thoughtless, for they may not have been the ones to come up with these ideas – which seem to reside within their domain of expertise.

When it comes to experts and the worth you bring to an innovation process, your real value comes in applying your knowledge and expertise to answering other people's questions, or issues related to their areas – not your own. This way you apply your mass of experience to seeing their issue differently – from your perspective – and so you can add value to the discussion that others can't. It's similar for the other experts around the table who will also be adding value to the discussion from their own area of expertise – but to other people's issues.

How many business growth questions have you been asked recently where the honest answer that you gave was that you didn't know? Most probably none. It's not the business protocol to ask this kind of question. And if you only came up with a certain idea for growth now – and it's a really simple and smart one – then why didn't you suggest this last year? In hindsight, it's often a no-win situation for the expert, which they subconsciously try to avoid by not asking the bold questions in the first place.

To correct this, we need to be asking questions that we don't know the answers to. Experts need to mentally change in a creative meeting from knowing everything, to knowing nothing – and to leave their expertise outside the door and become explorers for a while. As an expert, you might not be comfortable with the idea of not showing your expertise, but you need to consider yourself to be the explorer, and to apply a broad array of knowledge to other people's issues. To be an explorer for them. Later on, when it comes time to shape the opportunities into deliverables, then you can re-engage and assert your expertise to help with the execution. Making this change to becoming an explorer is hard – but very effective. Being an inexperienced explorer and avoiding commenting on your own area of expertise is one of the most effective ways for you to deliver greater degrees of innovation in your business.

Being too keen to answer the question

Additionally, because we as experts may be unwilling to explore, or don't have time to explore, we settle for the first best answer – and here's an example. When you lose your keys where do you always find them? The answer is in the last place you looked! That's because once you've found the solution to your quest – you stop looking. You can't find your keys again when they're already in your hand. But when you are trying to be innovative and find some alternative answer, it's different. Once you find one brilliant opportunity you must look even harder, because this shows how you've broken through the barrier of the obvious into new and uncharted ground, and more opportunities will undoubtedly exist close-by – but only if you continue to look and explore.

Unfortunately, and as we've seen, exploration does not come naturally to the expert. Once a good solution has been found to a question, then we like to move on to the next question – rather than move on to the next answer. When the expert stops looking, the explorer continues looking. For powerful questions have many different answers – not just one.

Cultural issues, too

And being British doesn't help either. Think of a workshop where there's a discussion on the growth a business could achieve by doing new things. The conversation covers a broad range of topics and for each one the appropriate expert is expected to spout forth words of wisdom in that area. By default, the expert will talk about what they know – not what they don't know. And in line with British cultural mandates, the other people in the room stay quiet, in deference to the expert at the table. But maybe things should be different.

When any specific topic is being discussed, and the people at the table are looking for fresh opportunities, perhaps the expert should be the one to shut up and so allow the rest of the people to talk. Because for innovation to happen, new things first need to be uncovered – and this is achieved through a process of exploration which is best done by those that don't know the area.

Demands on our time

Every organisation in business today is facing a wide range of demanding issues. Externally there are the state of the economic cycle, environmental requirements, increasingly restrictive legislation around many aspects of business and the risk from IT security issues – and an increasingly short-term focus on delivering results, to name just a few.

Internally there are over-worked employees in downsized companies trying to solve ever more complex situations, with smarter, more empowered, demanding and frequently sceptical customers expecting amazing service across many channels and devices – all wanting responses immediately on a 24/7 basis wherever they are.

Email, mobile phones, wearable devices, personal computers, automated systems, better transportation and telecommunications have all made productivity so much more efficient. We can work from home through secure virtual private networks and use a myriad of conferencing and collaboration tools to make our work more effective from almost any location in the world.

We're eating our five-a-day of fruit and veggies, not drinking and driving, and smoking less tobacco such that our life expectancy is steadily on the increase. We are getting fitter through exercise and lifestyle assisting gadgets, and chronic illness and previously debitating medical conditions are now under control, while dreaded diseases like cancer are irrevocably being beaten. We are able to continue working when many of our forebears would have had to give up work altogether.

Things are so much better now in so many ways – but there's only so much time in a day. We are permanently connected through our mobiles and tablets and so are always on, no matter where we are. Software tools enable others to access our calendars and to schedule us into meetings with every working hour seemingly being double- or triple-booked.

The speed of business is beginning to outstrip the speed of our thinking. Fortunately, for the moment, there's so much new material being developed that broad thinking and delivery expertise is enough to make it work, but the core fundamentals aren't right. Environmentally and socially we are reaching critical tipping points that may irreversibly change the planet and our societies. Some of our business and commercial activities too are putting our global economy at risk. We need to re-focus on some of the bigger issues that need a deeper level of thinking but there's no planned time for quality thinking. No off-time or down-time when we can allow our minds the freedom to think like a philosopher of old and to just contemplate on useful and interesting matters again.

But also, there are other reasons that good thinking doesn't flow naturally . . .

Why individuals struggle to be creative

In the 1960s, creativity researcher Dr George Land was approached by NASA to assess the creativity of the engineers they employed. The methodology he used worked so well for NASA that he started to apply it to children to assess the degree of creative genius they possessed. He tested the same children at five-year intervals to see if it changed over time, and these were the astonishing findings he uncovered:

- At 3–5 years of age, 98 per cent of children were rated as creative geniuses.

- At 8–10 years of age, only 32 per cent of *the same* children still rated as creative geniuses.
- At 13–15 years of age only 10 per cent were so rated.
- By the age of 25 and above, only 2 per cent of them were rated as creative geniuses.

The reason for this decline in creativity is believed to be that, as growing human beings, we are raised to conform to a wide range of norms, whereas young children are permitted much more freedom. While this may not be considered a critical issue for the majority of businesses who aren't involved in the design or creative industries, it turns out there are other similar issues in these creative industries too.

iStock (part of Getty Images) are an online provider of digital imagery and photographs, and in August 2013 they commissioned KRC Research to conduct a survey of over 400 young, creative professionals across the United States and United Kingdom ranging from art directors to graphic designers. Their published findings showed some unexpected and alarming results.

- 48 per cent believed the levels of creativity in their industry had stagnated or declined in the last decade.
- 23 per cent spent less than two hours of their day doing 'creative' work.
- 63 per cent said they don't have the time they need for 'creative reflection and inspiration'.
- Only 34 per cent rated the workplace as one of their top three locations for creativity.

If our creative professionals are struggling to produce inventive and effective solutions in an increasingly stressful work environment, what about other industries when their managers need to be creative in some way?

It's also interesting that the 'over-25' group that was identified by George Land are the junior to mid-level managers responsible for running large parts of any business today.

So what about those few times in a year when there's a real need for creative thinking to open up a new opportunity or to solve a difficult problem? These are the times when our over-25s need to step up to the plate and create – not conform. But are they able to achieve this? If the creative professionals are struggling to achieve their desired levels of creativity, what are we doing to assist our managers in this area?

Often, when people realise that as individuals they don't have the creative nouse to find a new answer, they may decide to involve a wider group of people to identify some new opportunities. The usual course of action may be to call a meeting where the attendees do some brainstorming. Unfortunately, this frequently doesn't address the issue as well as one might expect – or it fails to add any practical value at all – and here's why . . .

Why the business world's favourite thinking tool is letting us down

It was 1953 when Alex Osborn's book *Applied Imagination* birthed brainstorming. It was a cutting-edge concept at the time. It thrived in the same corporate environment alongside accounting's hand-cranked adding machine and marketing's action list written in chalk on the blackboard in the director's office.

The earliest investigations into the effectiveness of brainstorming happened at Yale University in 1958 – just five years after the process was developed. The surprising findings were that 48 solo participants had roughly twice as many ideas as 48 participants formed into brainstorming groups. A panel of judges also regarded the individuals' ideas to be more feasible and effective than those from the groups.

Over fifty years later in 2012, Keith Sawyer, a psychologist from Washington University, summarised the findings on brainstorming by saying: 'Decades of research have consistently shown that brainstorming groups think of far fewer ideas than the same number of people who work alone and later pool their ideas.'

If you find that brainstorming frequently fails on its promise to deliver, you're not alone. When six people have spent two hours in a room and plastered the walls with scores of sticky-notes – what's left at the end? Rarely the amazing new idea that was hoped for. Conventional brainstorming is a terrible waste of good people's time, because it works contrary to what is required to deliver exceptional business thinking. While a brainstorming group will get more ideas than any individual ever could working on their own, it's an inefficient and fundamentally flawed process.

Let's start by looking at the traditional guidelines for brainstorming to see why they don't work.

#1 There are no dumb ideas so encourage wild and exaggerated thinking

There are plenty of dumb ideas. Everyone in a brainstorming session knows that many of the ideas that are created will be impractical, way beyond the scope of the issue, too risky, not aligned to the company values or business aims – and so on. Wild and exaggerated ideas aren't intentionally stupid ideas, they're just totally impractical, pie-in-the-sky stuff – so they might as well be termed 'dumb'.

#2 Quantity counts at this stage, not quality

No, it doesn't. Quality is always important. Fewer ideas but with a better sense of quality will always be of more value than a large number of useless ideas.

#3 Don't criticise other people's ideas

There's limited time available in any creative thinking session, and if someone is being consistently unrealistic, then wouldn't a little constructive guidance help them to potentially create the one idea that's being looked for within the likely acceptable zone? Is there any other aspect of business where we encourage people to be wrong? Not offering guidance is a clear failure of any process.

#4 Build on other people's ideas

Sometimes useful, but often it can start adding weight and credence to an idea that wouldn't have made the grade if someone hadn't started to build on it.

#5 Every person and every idea has equal worth

No! Everyone has an equal opportunity to contribute something useful. How they use that time is up to them. Allowing people to wander too far into la-la-land starts to waste their chance for meaningful contributions – and it can also start to lead other people's thinking astray too.

#6 Create a fun environment

The future growth of your company often depends on these brainstorming sessions – so do you think that fun is at the forefront of your Board of Directors' collective mind? Children need to have fun. Serious professionals relish the chance to stretch their brains. There'll be more overall satisfaction among the participants if they sense a successful outcome rather than them having a fun time creating nothing of practical value.

#7 Only one person talking at a time

When you're trying to concentrate on some important thinking issue, do you find it useful to have someone blabbing? Especially when you are supposed to be paying attention to what they're saying? Doubtful. Your best ideas frequently come when you have moments of silence to consider the issue in your mind. This brainstorming rule ensures that there may only be one person talking at a time – but also that there's *always* someone talking.

So the basic principles of a brainstorming session are flawed. But that's not all. There are other deeper issues that cause problems too.

#8 HiPPOs rule the waves

The highest paid person's opinion (HiPPO) openly and subconsciously influences what success will look like. What they offer in the way of ideas, how they comment on the ideas of others, and the slow-nodding of their head in agreement when they hear a good idea. HiPPOs adversely affect what people say and do in brainstorming sessions. Having a HiPPO in the room can also limit what ideas people voice for fear of making a career-limiting move through the suggestion of an idea which the HiPPO may regard negatively.

#9 Accepting the lowest common denominator

Rather than allowing a motivated individual to develop a feasible idea that they feel passionate about, a brainstorming group often promotes the idea that they feel most comfortable with. This is the lowest common denominator of agreement, which isn't necessarily of the highest value or potential. It's similar to agreeing to just take the low-hanging fruit, which invariably consists of lesser, and easier ideas to execute. While the brainstorming group is promoting the lowest common denominator as their recommendation – the best opportunity for the business may invariably be left as a sticky-note on the wall – as it's deemed too high up on the fruit tree.

#10 False anchoring

Early in the session, somebody puts up an idea which gets a supportive comment like 'that's brilliant'. This is a recipe for disaster, for from that moment on, this idea acts as a false anchor or a black hole for thinking. Similarly with a HiPPO's comment too. The early ideas in a session frequently tend to get prominence, as people openly (or inadvertently) state their pet idea with some supporting comment designed to influence people. The early ideas (if they are strong) tend to define the terrain and also form immovable anchors. Additionally, people who are the acknowledged experts in their field will invariably tend to provide artificial anchor points through the ideas they voice in a group.

#11 Aggression or agreement

If a team is involved in brainstorming an issue, they are generally encouraged to sit around being supportive and reaching a consensus. However pleasant and warming it may feel, in-breeding isn't a desirable trait to encourage. Teams need to get outsiders in to challenge their thinking. This is contrary to the brainstorming approach where a team want to be seen to be getting along. Potentially, it's during this search for new opportunities where the existing 'pleasant stability' needs to be most strongly challenged.

#12 Voting on ideas

Frequently at the end of a brainstorm, people vote on the best ideas to take forward. Unless the team are all responsible for the success of the outcome, the choice of what to do next should be left to the owner of the issue. They, as the responsible person, should decide in the light of a new day what will be taken forward. In longer ideation sessions that have an overnight break, it's remarkable how often the priorities identified at the end of the previous day change as a result of the overnight subconscious of the participants being given time to influence – without any formal exercises being done. If a brainstorming group vote on the best idea in a session, it's demoralising for them when a single person has to override their decision at a later stage.

#13 The illusion of productivity

A group of people working towards the same company goals will invariably feel that their combined skills, knowledge and abilities working in a brainstorming session will have added value to the business. The aforementioned lowest common denominator effect potentially means that they will deliver outputs lower than their potential to achieve. Unfortunately this starts reinforcing beliefs that mediocrity is deemed to be success – and that the process has been successful.

#14 Group hugs

At the end of a session, it's customary for the sponsor to thank people and be complimentary about the output. If six people have been in the meeting, five will walk out having been warmly thanked by the sixth, and feel that they've added value in the time they gave up. The sponsor, meanwhile, is left to try and pull some magic out of a sticky-note hat. One unhappy person, five happy – and the myth of another valuable brainstorming session is perpetuated within the business.

So what now?

Times may have changed and the adding machines and blackboards are sitting in landfill sites or in museums, but shockingly, thinking about growth opportunities frequently still depends on brainstorming.

There are reasons today why we are old-fashioned thinkers. It's because we know no different, and also because we allow ourselves to be guided by others who know no different than brainstorming. Brainstorming is always well-meaning and intuitively feels like the right thing to do – and some benefits may accrue as it gets people in the same room and talking about an issue which they wouldn't normally do otherwise.

The year 2018 will be a year for celebration, as brainstorming will be 65 years old – the official retirement age in many businesses. However, any company that is serious in its need for better growth opportunities should retire it earlier. Like right now! Brainstorming is a broken model with too much ineffective momentum locked in for it to be turned around. It's an inefficient thinking process which needs to be replaced with a new approach that is based upon our contemporary knowledge of how the mind works.

Brainstorming encourages passive thinking – a peaceful, wait-your-turn, unbounded type of thinking. Unfortunately for brainstorming, business growth needs something better – and today is as good a day as any to put brainstorming out of its misery. It's time for a 21st century approach to thinking. A more aggressive, focused and stimulating approach that will help businesses to out-think their competition.

It's time for *The Idea Generator* to deliver a new thinking approach for you.

A new way of business thinking

There are five generic types of thinking we use in the work environment depending on the specific situation being considered at any given moment. We may use analytical thinking to evaluate a range of options; intuitive thinking to respond to an issue without having full awareness of the facts; executional thinking to organise our knowledge into a plan that can be carried out; or conceptual thinking where we assemble data or components to reveal a pattern or a bigger picture. And then there's creative thinking – the kind of thinking that identifies the new and previously unseen solution or opportunity.

The vast majority of daily thinking activity (outside of the direct creative industries) is concerned with analytical, intuitive, executional or conceptual thinking. For business people it's often your previous successes with these types of thinking that produced and delivered the successes that fill up your résumé – and which probably got you employed in your current role in the first place.

Sometimes, however, best practice isn't good enough or appropriate to the situation, and at these times you desire to identify a different practice. Something novel. New. Previously unseen. And this is where some creative thinking is needed. This is likely to be a relatively small part of your role – but when it's needed, it can deliver massive benefits for your company and for you personally too.

The previous chapter showed that despite all the challenges we face in the work environment, our thinking is the one area in business that is being left behind – which is peculiar, as it's probably the most important skill we possess in the workplace. So how can we cope with the additional thinking that is required of us? We'd all love to be able to instantly develop our brains to think in a speedier fashion and to increase our neural capacity to allow us to resolve multi-dimensional systems issues in our heads. But unfortunately we can't. Therefore we need to change what we can change, and that's our approach to business thinking – and the way we actually think. You can advance your thinking abilities by using The Idea Generator as your support mechanism and driving force.

So, what is The Idea Generator? The Idea Generator is three things. It's a book you read; it's a process you adopt; and finally it's the person you become. For The Idea Generator is what you can aspire to be – and what your business needs you to be. There is no downside to being The Idea Generator, for you'll be a person that a business always needs – because you are the one who can produce winning ideas.

Winning ideas

Some executives may state they don't need more ideas, as they've got enough good ideas in the business already. But if a business has ideas that they aren't implementing, then they aren't good ideas at all – they're just clutter that's choking up the corporate sphincter.

Great ideas are the ideal answers to important questions. When a company has lots of ideas, these may well be wonderful answers to interesting questions – but unfortunately they aren't the questions that anyone is asking in the business. This may be due to the fact that the questions are being regarded as ones which aren't worth asking in the current environment, or that there are more appropriate and valuable questions that need to be addressed instead.

Paris, 11 and helium are perfect general knowledge answers. But only if the questions being asked are what's the capital of France, the square root of 121 and the chemical element represented by the symbol He. Otherwise they are useless answers – and of no value at all. Just like the ideas clogging up your business by appearing to be of value. If an idea isn't being executed then it needs to be evacuated from the business bowel and flushed away so that it doesn't confuse people with its appearance of false value.

Winning ideas are those opportunities or solutions that address a specific and significant question that's currently being asked in the business. They are timely to a current business issue.

However, just because an idea answers a current question doesn't mean it's a winning idea, for it could be a ridiculous and totally impractical course of action to take. Winning ideas are grounded in the capabilities of the business to deliver them. Even though the idea may not be a fully fleshed-out solution, it appears to be do-able within the anticipated constraints of the business and is relevant and meaningful to the overall aims of the business. There have been plenty of great ideas in the past which would have been roaring successes if the business had budgets of billions and timeframes of decades to deliver them. Unfortunately, this is rarely the case. So winning ideas are always grounded in the realistic constraints of a given situation.

Additionally, winning ideas are not necessarily about being the definitive and complete answer to a given situation. They are ideas that win people over to a way of thinking or an initial approach. Winning ideas are those that people are interested in getting behind and supporting or assisting with. They tend to form an immediate team of interested volunteers, or a community with a common goal or interest in achieving a future situation. They allow others to flex them, and to add to them, so these other people feel they are part of the development of the optimum solution.

Winning ideas leave room for others to get on-board which helps build momentum towards a winning solution or opportunity. Winning ideas don't have to be over-sold and their cause argued resolutely for, because they appear to others as the natural next step to take. Winning ideas win people over by default, and The Idea Generator is your way to winning ideas.

Killer Questions and Querencia

All thinking can be boiled down into one of two opposing categories. Thinking about what you know and thinking about what you don't know. What you know is your knowledge, expertise and skills and massively occupies the biggest chunk of your thinking. It's the 'vast majority' of your thinking time that was mentioned previously. The tiny remainder of your thinking time is focused on what you don't know.

Here's a question for you. How much time did you spend thinking about what you don't know today? What about this week? Probably not much. And yet what you don't know far outweighs what you do know in the same degree as the size of the universe to the size of Earth. The real value for yourself, your business – and even society as a whole – is when you think about something you don't know and convert it into something you do know. Because then you can implement something that adds value. This conversion of what you don't know into what you do know is where asking questions comes in – but not just any type of question.

To identify big and bold opportunities, a business needs to be asking big and bold questions – or Killer Questions. They're the sort of questions that experts and many leaders are fearful of asking because the immediate response to a 'How do we achieve (this goal)?' Killer Question is possibly made up of the three most feared words in the business lexicon: 'I don't know.' But these are the challenging questions that break new ground. They are the questions that need answering and that we shouldn't fear asking. These are the questions that help us to align our thinking in a specific, new and desirable direction. These are the questions that help us to find our Querencia.

Querencia is a lovely Spanish word from the bull-fighting world. It doesn't have a direct translation into English, but the approximate translation is 'the place of safety that the bull retreats to before launching its final charge'. The place from which there is only one direction to go – and that's forward.

To undertake powerful thinking it's important to back yourself into a place mentally, so that you are absolutely sure that when you start your thinking activities, you are heading in the best direction. Whether you are working alone or as a team, don't start any thinking exercise until you are absolutely sure that your chosen direction is where you need to go. When you find your Querencia, there's no need to look left or right. No looking over your shoulder. You focus on going forward, because your success lies only in that direction. One of the easiest ways of finding Querencia is to start off with a well-formed question – your Killer Question. This way you (or all of you if you are part of a group) are absolutely committed to forging ahead in the direction of achieving a specific goal, which is the answer to your Killer Question.

When your question is in Querencia – when it's shaped into a form that all involved agree and support – then there's only one way for it to go. Forward. No distractions – for your question is ready to be answered. But what makes a great Killer Question?

Killer Question development

A Killer Question gets people's attention. Whether it's due to the zone of opportunity it is targeted at, its ambitious nature, or the fact of the newness or novelty of a question that's not been asked before is irrelevant. People recognise that it's a question that's desirable to ask for the benefit of the business.

Killer Questions can sometimes shock people by their remarkable focus, or amaze them due to their awesomeness. Let's look at two extreme examples from two extreme scenarios.

In the 2005 Nicolas Cage film *Lord of War*, Cage plays an arms dealer who provides a narration over the start of the film. He states that there are over 550 million firearms in worldwide circulation which represents one firearm for every 12 people on the planet. Cage's character then poses the Killer Question: 'So how do we arm the other eleven?' This is a question designed to shock due entirely to its profoundly focused (though extremely negative) nature.

Another Killer Question was posed by Facebook's Mark Zuckerberg recently: 'How can we make the Internet one hundred times more affordable?' The reasoning behind this is that two-thirds of the world's population does not have access to the Internet, and Zuckerberg and a coalition of mobile technology companies want to change this. They want to bring the Internet to every single person on Earth who has a mobile phone. The consortium that hope to achieve this is called Internet.org and exactly how and when Internet.org will attain their goal is yet to be finalised. However, the vision of reducing the cost 100-fold is an awesomely bold question.

A Killer Question in business is when you ask a question that hasn't formally been asked before, but which is actually a really powerful question to pose. A question that won't be easy to answer, but if answered well, has the potential to deliver huge value for the business. However, as was previously stated, asking questions like this isn't a part of human nature – and neither is it a normal part of business nature. The unfortunate thing is that when it comes to questions, we are actually taught to take the easy option. In an exam where you have a choice of questions, it's always the best thing to choose the easier ones or the ones that you know how to answer. And this makes sense because when a lot is at stake, who is going to choose the harder options?

When a business wants to do something innovative, it should be something that has a high degree of difficulty to it. Why? Because when you successfully answer a difficult question, it makes it harder for the competition to copy you. It also stops you repeating the same old easy answers over and over as well.

So, to trigger some innovative opportunities for growth, you start by asking a bold, new Killer Question. It's a natural trait to be concerned about how you will answer this Killer Question, but you mustn't worry about the answers at this stage. All you want to do is to get a great question and to get a few people interested in supporting that question as one that is well worth asking. Accept the fact that at the end of this question and answer process your thinking exercise will be measured on the success of your outputs. On finding the right answers. But the more important thing to focus on right now is whether you know the right question to ask. For in business, there's no profit or glory in finding perfect answers to the wrong question.

To ensure you get the kind of outputs your business needs, it's essential to interrogate your question first. To question your question. To give it a good kicking to ensure that before you even consider answering it, you are certain it's the best possible question for you to spend your valuable time and thinking efforts on.

Once you have formed your draft question, write it down to prevent it from changing itself inside your mind. Then use these five interrogation approaches to give you confidence that the question you want to ask will be of big value to your business – that it will be the Killer Question you should be asking.

1. Is it meaningful?

Is your question aligned to the strategic direction of the business and/or your department? Does it add value for the customer? Is it addressing an issue that is acknowledged within your business – or is this something that you personally have on your agenda? The more meaningful and aligned to the business aims that your question is, and the more it is focused on addressing a customer-related issue, then the more support you will have when you identify interesting outcomes.

2. Is it pragmatic?

Are the outputs from your question likely to be within the available constraints of time, effort and money that are available to you? While you may need to request additional resources to execute the outputs – are they reasonable given the scale of the potential benefits that will be generated? And if your outputs have to compete with other initiatives for funding, how likely is it that the answers to your question will be high enough on the agenda to be allocated those limited resources?

3. Does it help address your superior's goals?

It's useful to ask questions that help you attain your own appraised goals for the year, but will this question (when successfully answered) also help your boss to achieve their goals? And their superior's goals too? If so, you have a much greater chance of gaining support for your question and resources for its answers.

Even the most amazing of output solutions or opportunities won't get implemented if they aren't aligned to the overall corporate goals, for this will be deflecting resources away from the items that are on individuals' performance measures to your requirements that aren't.

4. Is it within your remit to deliver?

Will the answers to this question be executed solely by you, your team, or by people under your control? If not, then potentially this question overlaps with another area of the business. To get buy-in to your eventual answers – get this other area's involvement with your question at the start. Then subsequently, they will have greater engagement with your outputs as they were part of forming the question. If you go ahead without their involvement from the beginning, you risk having them disagree with your initial question when you want their participation in executing the answers.

However, if the question is entirely within your remit, then you have full control over the shaping of the question and the subsequent delivery of the outputs.

5. Does it answer the 'So what?' test?

Here's a quick check you can carry out called the 'So what?' test. Next time you are thinking on an issue, imagine that you come up with a great idea to address that issue. Now ask yourself, 'So what?' Will this make a big difference to your world or the issue? If the answer isn't a resounding yes – then why are you doing it? Find a bigger and better issue to apply your mental capabilities to. We often tend to clutter our lives, our heads and our thinking with issues that aren't important. Just focus on the big issues. Keep asking yourself, 'So what?' This will help keep you focused on the big stuff.

By using these five checks to interrogate your Killer Question before you answer it, you'll ensure that you have achieved Querencia and will save yourself a lot of potentially wasted effort if people disagree with your question later.

You may think that some of these five checks should be applied to the output ideas rather than the initial question – but not so. Even though you don't know what the final output idea or ideas will be, these checks help you to ensure that whatever solutions arise, they will be of value in the bigger scheme of things.

Also, by sharing your question with others earlier in the process, it's a chance for them to get buy-in to your aims. Some people may just want to see the outputs of your thinking exercise and assist with their execution and delivery if they deem them to be strong and valuable. Others may prefer to be involved in the actual answering of the Killer Question itself, which is definitely of benefit to you as this is more early support and assistance with the thinking process. And subsequently by default they will be more supportive and engaged with the outputs of the project too.

Examples of great Killer Questions

Your Killer Questions will likely fall into one of the three categories that The Idea Generator toolsets cover, so here are some example Killer Questions from a number of industries in each category.

Category 1: A new thinking project

- **The marketing department:** How can we include items in our marketing interactions with customers that would trigger them to talk positively about our ABC product (or us) on social media and so boost the levels of word-of-mouth advocacy?
- **Public services head of human resources:** We are commencing with a major new transformation process shortly, so how can we creatively engage people in the process so they see it as a benefit for them rather than a drain on their time?
- **A small business owner:** What are some innovative things we can do as a business that will make us more appealing to be acquired by a larger company within three years?

Category 2: Revisiting an old problematic area

- **A book publishing company:** How can we re-purpose the huge collection of titles that we own to create additional revenues without committing to major expenditure?

- **A membership-based organisation:** How can we get a 33 per cent uplift in new members this year by repositioning the value we offer and the benefits of being a member?

- **A high street retail business:** What are some bold moves we can make to counteract the decline in our sales and footfall due to the trend towards online shopping over the next 12 months?

Category 3: Looking for growth opportunities

- **A telecommunications company:** What are some ways we can extend our home-based services such that they have intrinsic appeal to the retired consumers where we have very low penetration?

- **A product head:** What are some relatively small changes we can make to our ABC product that will enable us to boost revenues significantly in the current financial year?

- **A customer retention manager:** How do we reduce our 19 per cent annual churn rate to below 10 per cent by applying innovative thinking to the big issues that our company and our industry face?

You'll notice that the Killer Questions are phrased in a positive manner and have targets attached which helps to keep people focused on the scale of success and the parameters of constraint that the ideal solutions should try to attain.

Here are some examples of poorly formed Killer Questions, and how they can be modified to be better.

- *Should we [DO THIS] or [DO THAT] to lift sales?* This assumes that a dilemma exists and there is only a choice between two options. It's likely that there are many more options to consider than just two, so this question could be rephrased as: *What innovative options do we have to guarantee we achieve our business targets for this financial year?*

- *How do we make the ABC product the solution to our sales problems?* This question is trying to force-fit a known item or idea into a solution. A better phrasing of this question would be: *How can we dramatically increase the revenues from our ABC products so that we achieve a sales increase of 25 per cent over last year's figures?*

Forming a Killer Question isn't a hard thing to do. Making sure it's the right Killer Question before you start to answer it takes a bit of effort. But once you are satisfied with your Killer Question and that it has placed you perfectly in Querencia, then you are ready to start. However, before you do actually start using the tools, it's important for you to be able to get yourself into The Idea Generator mindset.

The Idea Generator mindset

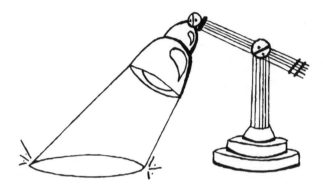

Thinking may seem an easy activity as you do it all the time. It's impossible not to think, as that in itself is a thinking act. But the real skill comes when you want to start thinking creatively with a purpose. While the phrase *creative thinking* may conjure up visions of lounging on beanbags and waiting for moments of inspiration or serendipity, this isn't the approach taken by The Idea Generator. When you have a desire to find an innovative new answer to a question, The Idea Generator takes a hardcore approach to thinking differently. You need to have a mindset that's committed to achieving your desired outcome and which embraces all the following aspects.

A structured approach

To ensure the delivery of valuable outcomes, The Idea Generator uses a highly structured approach to creativity. There's no staring into space with a big sheet of blank paper and some coloured pens in front of you. Like a thoroughbred race horse, your creativity needs to be tightly harnessed and ridden hard over a pre-determined course. This course is formed by a proven set of tools and techniques to ensure the desired outcomes are obtained.

With The Idea Generator you start by selecting the toolset that's most appropriate to the type of issue you are considering, and then you use the individual techniques within the toolset to explore a variety of situations related to your issue. The tools themselves are structured to lead your thinking on an optimal route that's most suited to driving out the results you need.

An example of how The Idea Generator approach differs from other techniques, is to consider how you might have previously been stimulated or encouraged to 'think outside of the box' in order to be creative. While at a high level this may seem like an appropriate course of action, unfortunately, there is so much that is outside of the box, that the vast majority is too far-fetched or impractical to be of use in the business environment. The Idea Generator toolsets create a series of well-structured boxes that are relevant to your issue and then orientates your thinking to deliver ideas that are inside of these boxes. The result is an array of ideas that are highly focused on a specific aspect of the issue – and not ideas that are spread thinly over vast regions of extraneous space.

Another example of the degree of structure inherent to The Idea Generator is that the toolsets take a project approach to thinking. In business, while much of the work is routine, some specific tasks are outside of the normal day-to-day activity and need to be treated differently – as projects. The Idea Generator treats all thinking exercises as specific thinking projects – and with good reason and effect. Projects have specific purposes and have a clearly defined starting point along with a set of outcomes or deliverables that need to happen. There is often a series of other over-arching constraints such as time, budget, resource limitations as well as a need to integrate with, or involve, other parties within the business or organisation. These are some key differentiators of projects from the regular business activities.

The thinking exercises that The Idea Generator offers are deliberately structured as projects with defined start and end points and a focus Killer Question. The process format helps to minimise scope creep, where thinking can start to wander off into areas that are less likely to contain solutions that will be considered as successful answers to the Killer Question. Note that evolution of your thinking within the scope of the project is advantageous and encouraged. However, if left unchecked, this can start to head off into strange areas and distract from the focus on achieving the stated end-goals of the project.

The three toolset templates that accompany this book contain guidelines to lead your mind through a clear process to think about your Killer Question differently, and also provide all the writing space and frameworks needed to use each tool. The templates also contain ideas assessment and development tools and act as a repository to keep all your thoughts and ideas conveniently in one place.

A desire to out-think yourself and others

When you outsmart someone, it's a you-win/they-lose scenario which may not deliver any overall benefit to anyone but yourself. However, when you are able to out-think someone, it's challenging to stretch your mind to think further and better than someone else has done before. It's an advancement of thinking on a given subject that doesn't cause harm to another party. It just encourages them to try and think harder by raising the overall thinking level around the topic.

But the best person to aim to out-think is yourself. When you get ideas on a specific thinking topic that are better than anything you've ever identified before – then you are out-thinking yourself. You've pushed yourself to achieve a higher level of thinking. If you are part of a team all thinking on the same topic, then a friendly challenge to come up with the best idea ensures that the final output is better than anything that could have been delivered with a less committed thinking effort.

When your interest in an exciting thinking project spurs your desire to out-think yourself and others, and this subsequently becomes a passion for you, then you will find yourself in an inspirational zone where you are on the upward spiral of success. And the only way to ensure you remain on this upward spiral is to keep this desire to become an ever-better thinker bubbling away inside yourself. Success breeds success and continued use of the toolsets will help you, The Idea Generator, to achieve that accomplishment initially – and to sustain it on an ongoing basis too.

This may sound like an obvious statement, but businesses don't think – individuals do. So whether you are an individual in a large corporate, a big organisation, a small business, or want to work alone on a personal or social issue – these techniques will work and help you to out-think yourself (and others) in any situation, and for any thinking project you define.

The ability to make time

Making time for your thinking is one of the hardest tasks that you'll have to manage. While some things can be multi-tasked – like reading a document while listening on a conference call – thinking isn't one of them. Great thinking needs its own focused and committed time for clear, undisturbed effort. Blocks of 15–30 minutes are often good to carve out of your day; however, when these blocks of time actually happen is also very important for you.

Many people feel they are at their most creative in the morning, before the daily toils of a business day have begun to wear them down and destroy their soul. Also, immediately prior to, or just after, a key meeting is not a good time, as your mind will suffer from attention residue where it will be pre-occupied either with the upcoming meeting or with the events that transpired in the last meeting. Try to block out your thinking time in the less hectic parts of your day or week.

Some useful times of the day are while on the train or bus when commuting to work – or you could head down to the coffee shop for a thinking-focused coffee break. For most people this time will need to be scheduled; however, if a block of time becomes free and you feel like some mental stimulation, then get your thinking issue ready and take it for a good work-out.

Obviously your ability to schedule thinking time very much depends on your position in the business and you may consider that the higher up the corporate ladder you are, the harder it is to take time off for thinking. An extreme example is Bill Gates who was renowned for taking Think-Weeks twice every year. He would spend these alone at a secret waterfront cottage in Washington State where he would think about the Microsoft business and what its future could be, without the fear of any disturbances.

The AMC award-winning television series *Mad Men* is set in the US advertising industry in the sixties and portrays some of the attitudes prevalent at the time. While many of their behaviours may seem quite appalling to today's work and home life, there was little technology beyond the electric typewriter and coffee percolator involved in the work environment. In one scene the lead character, Don Draper, is sat in a chair staring at the wall, thinking, and his boss walks into his office, sees this and comments, 'I never get used to the fact that you always seem to be doing nothing.' People had so much more time for thinking 50 years ago – and this was the environment in which brainstorming was developed.

When it comes to carving out thinking time, you'll need to be ruthless and create gaps that suit the way and time that you prefer to think. Unfortunately, being ruthless is your only likely option for success in this regard.

Knowing your place

Once you've made time available, you'll need to find a place to do your thinking, and the best places are where you aren't normally found. If you stay at your desk, you'll probably be approached by people who think you are working and that it's okay to interrupt you. So break your pattern and go somewhere else – either inside your building or outside of it.

If you want to stay inside your building, go to the café (if you have one) or go to another floor where you won't be found or noticed and grab a space for a while. If you decide to go out somewhere, a park or quiet place like a library is ideal – but these locations aren't close to many people's offices. However, coffee shops are. Find one that's not frequented by people from your office and take a seat – preferably one with few distractions. People walking in and out are a distraction, so stay away from the door, and if needed face the wall so you aren't interrupted. If there's a quiet corner that can act as a hideaway, then so much the better.

For some people the perfect thinking time is while exercising – running, at the gym on the treadmill or cycling. Just make sure you have some way of capturing your ideas such as a dictaphone or a voice recording app on your smartphone. Whatever location you use, you'll need some way of noting down your ideas so that you can add them into your template later. If you are going to be thinking while exercising or doing some other activity, like driving a long distance, know what your issue is from your template before you start and focus on that for the duration of your exercise or journey.

For others, home is the best place for thinking. Either after the family has gone to bed, or more likely, before they wake up. Charles Dickens was a daylight man who did his creative writing between nine in the morning and two in the afternoon. Franz Kafka was a night man who wrote from eleven at night through to six the next morning. Philosopher Immanuel Kant wrote between six and seven in the morning, while Kingsley Amis worked from nine in the morning until one and then again between five and seven in the evening. You need to know when your most creative time is – and play to that strength. You are only doing very short sprints compared to these authors, so timing is more important for you. Experiment and learn – and then use your best time.

Having a strong focus

Your Killer Question is the overall focus issue that's important for you and your business and so is worthy of the effort you are going to apply. Knowing it's of value to your business and that you have the authority to initiate delivery or have a route to position it into the right person or area can also help you to focus from a self-motivational aspect.

Each of the tools within the toolset is designed to help you focus on one specific aspect or approach to the issue under consideration. When you are working with a tool, another self-driver is to decide to complete the tool before you take a break. Or, as some of the tools allow you to take numerous bites of the same cherry, decide how many cycles you want to attempt and commit to completing that number before you finish.

Being focused on the commitment of time and effort is equally as important as the actual issue you focus on, for the longer you spend thinking on an issue with appropriate stimuli and process, the greater the chance of finding the amazing outcome you are looking for. When thinking on a topic with passion and gusto, then your commitment will be reinforced with every exciting idea you develop.

Getting an attitude

To become The Idea Generator you need to get an attitude to your thinking. Actually, you need two attitudes – an external one and an internal one.

You know how short of time you are in the business environment, so when you create some precious time in your day, you need to ensure you push back and prevent people from taking it away from you. These distractions by people can involve asking you to do something else in this time or it can be trying to get your attention while you are actively thinking. For the relatively short periods of your day when you are doing your thinking, look busy – act as if there's a huge DO NOT DISTURB sign hanging right above your head. Put your headphones on and listen to some instrumental music that calms your mind and blocks out the hubbub of the area around you. If you are interrupted by something that breaks your thinking flow, acknowledge it as briefly as you can and get back inside your head. Turn up your DO NOT DISTURB sign a little brighter.

The internal attitude that you create is the one of absolute commitment to what you are thinking about. Go deep into your mind with the tool and don't hold back. If you were physically exerting yourself it's usually not the best thing to 'go for broke' as you may injure yourself. It's important to be in control with exercise such that you are giving your muscles a good work-out but you aren't damaging or destroying yourself. Thinking is different. You can 'go for broke' without any risk of injury. Push the boundaries of the box you are thinking into and go a little beyond the limits when you are being creative – the effort won't do you any harm at all. If the ideas start to get a little weird, then there's an opportunity later to tone them down, but while you are thinking, know that this could be of real value to you. Just one idea is all you need as the trigger starting point of a new solution or opportunity train of thought. Go for it and don't hold back. This is the internal attitude that you deserve to have and need to have.

Sometimes this attitude can be induced through the use of a ritual. Doing your thinking at your ideal time, in your preferred place, with a certain kind of music playing in your headphones, and with a particular drink you enjoy. Repeated use of the same ritual will help you to get into your optimal thinking zone more quickly, so try to maximise your ritual's elements so they work perfectly to help get you deep into your thinking.

If you're in a coffee shop, order a large coffee – even with an extra shot. The caffeine kick will stimulate your thinking, and you deserve a large coffee – because it takes longer to drink and so extends your justifiable thinking time there! And this is potentially the most valuable bit of work you will do all day (possibly even in your entire life – you'll never know) so don't feel guilty.

All mobile phones come with an OFF button – so use it while you do your thinking. A switched-off phone is better than a muted or silent one, as vibrations and screens lighting up will always get your attention and distract you from your thinking purpose. It's setting up the mechanisms in your mind that once the coffee is in the cup, the pen is in the hand hovering over the relevant template, and your head goes down – you become engrossed in your task. That's when you become The Idea Generator.

To really boost your thinking attitude to a higher level there are some additional thinking skills you can develop and master. They aren't essential, but they will help you become more effective in your thinking.

Making and breaking connections

All ideas are created from other ideas, thoughts or knowledge that you have. An interesting thought is applied to a piece of knowledge that you have and this combination triggers a new connection – which becomes a fresh idea for you. This is all based on the patterns of neurons that fire in sequences in your brain. Follow the same old route of thinking and the same old sequence of neurons fire – which deliver the same old ideas. For new ideas to form you have to force different sequences of neurons to fire – and this is achieved by connecting un-usual or new combinations of things inside your mind. Posing yourself a Killer Question which is something you haven't considered before is a great start, as already this is a source of a whole set of different considerations for your business and for your mind.

The benefit of making new connections is two-fold: by making the new connections, you are simultaneously breaking the old, established connections – which breaks you free of your existing thinking patterns, which is precisely what creative thinking is.

The use of The Idea Generator and the tools in the templates is a spe-cifically crafted process designed to force new ways of thinking, and by default the use of the templates will encourage new connections to be forged. Some of the great scientists, philosophers and engineers of our time who break new ground are those that know how to stimulate new mental connections. When new neurons start firing across syn-apses that have never been used before you are literally getting mental breakthroughs. So to encourage these breakthroughs, load up the inputs and force the neurons to wake up and fire to get new outputs.

A simple example of how to stimulate new connections is to have your Killer Question, or the focus subject of one of the tools on the tem-plates, and to match that to known situations elsewhere. As long as the combination of the two things you are trying to connect is differ-ent to what you've always considered before, then the chances of a breakthrough idea occurring are much improved.

Engaging your subconscious

Your subconscious is a very powerful ally when it comes to thinking. You may have had an idea come to you 'out of the blue' while driving, out walking or even in the shower. You weren't thinking of the issue at the time, but a relevant and meaningful idea seemed to blurt itself out in your mind. That's your subconscious at work. You clearly had an issue that you had previously been thinking about and although you'd switched off your active thinking processes, the subconscious ones were still running in the background.

Your Killer Question is the focus of your thinking project and it's important to have this sitting in your subconscious. You may well find that spurious ideas related to your Killer Question come to you at random times of the day or night. The important thing is to value your subconscious outputs and to capture them before they are forgotten – which happens surprisingly easily. Even some of the unusual techniques in the templates will cause other stimulating issues to be embedded within your subconscious – so encourage it to deliver more for you by valuing and capturing the output it surreptitiously delivers for you.

Employing a greater awareness

Your Killer Question is like a magnet – it attracts things towards it. And this is the beauty and the power of a Killer Question. Things that you have noticed or considered before now take on a new relevance, meaning, purpose and use when you look at them through the lens of your Killer Question. The fact that you see these common and known things differently is a powerful source of new triggers and ideas. And similarly, things that may be new to you are also considered through the Killer Question lens and so are of immediate relevance and opportunity.

Involving others

Even though you are fully engaged with your thinking project, others on the periphery (or even not involved at all) can still add value for you. People who are directly involved with your business add the value of an alternative viewpoint from within the project, while 'outsiders' who aren't involved at all can give you impromptu insights and perspectives when you probe them with a relevant and interesting question. Sometimes it's quite impressive what a second brain can offer as it sees things very differently to how you see them. Leverage an outsider's ignorance of your issue to deliver instant value into your project and to act as a trigger for your own thinking.

Mindset summary

Here's a summary of what you need to have to embrace The Idea Generator's mindset:

- A structured approach
- A desire to out-think yourself and others
- The ability to make time
- Knowing your place
- Getting an attitude

Also, the following skills:

- Making and breaking connections
- Engaging your subconscious
- Employing a greater awareness
- Involving others

When you embrace these components, then you have The Idea Generator's mindset and are primed to begin using the tools to their best effect.

Using the tools

The Idea Generator is an innovative approach to thinking about important issues. It consists of three specific toolsets for different types of issues and each toolset incorporates five novel thinking tools. Because you will be applying these toolsets for the first time to achieve successful outcomes for some of your ambitious thinking projects, it's important for you to understand how the process and the tools work. This short chapter will give you an overview of this.

Why pen and paper?

The thinking tools that form The Idea Generator are formatted for the use of a pen and paper approach. While this may sound a bit of a backward step given all the technology that we have around us, there's good reasoning behind it. Pen and paper is the best method for capturing ideas quickly and automatically. It allows words, sketches, diagrams, flows, processes and anything else to be captured easily, and rapidly, on paper. Some items can be captured in a semi-automatic mode too – if you want to write a short sentence down you don't have to think about it too much as your hand can almost write basic content on its own. It can even draw arrows and simple flows or diagrams without too much thought. And this is important for if you have to put too much thought into writing, then it tends to break up your creative thinking flow.

With any technology, the tapping of keys to enter text starts to detract and distract from the creative flow, especially when you also start changing what you've written, formatting it and correcting spelling mistakes. All these 'helpful' things that the technology assists you to do actually interrupt the creative flow. Not so with pen and paper.

You'll notice that many good designers carry a notebook around with them, and the perennial favourite is the Moleskine brand. This is because it enables them to capture notes, concepts and sketches as and when they come to them – and as all good designers know, inspiration can occur at any moment without warning. As the ideas need to be captured immediately, a notebook is the ideal medium. It's also different to what most people do. For many in the work environment, most of their mental output is captured directly into a digital format through the use of a technology of some kind. Creating an email, doing a calculation, sending a text message, even when 'speaking' to someone using instant messaging – all done without the use of paper.

Using a paper-based approach for your creative thinking is deliberately different – and this difference is beneficial as it supports you in the way your mind likes to flow when it thinks. This paper format approach is set out in the form of templates that help guide your thinking and which can be used to capture all your output.

A templated approach

There are three toolset templates to download, one for each category of thinking project:

1 **Islands of Opportunity** helps you efficiently identify opportunities to an issue which is new or hasn't been tackled before.

2 **Divide and Conquer** is intended to consider a more difficult issue that has probably been addressed before but which is still unresolved and which needs fresh thinking.

3 **Boundary Riding** is specifically structured to identify multiple growth opportunities within (or near to) your current business areas.

The templates can be downloaded free of charge from **www. TheIdeaGenerator.info**

Each of these templates is fully self-contained with all the components you'll need to complete your thinking project. All you need to do when starting a project is to download the appropriate PDF template and print it out.

Each template contains five specific tools that are relevant to the particular category of thinking project being undertaken and each tool contains specific areas to write your ideas in as you progress through the process. The final part of the template contains a section to help you assess the best ideas and build and boost them to a higher level. Once you've finished with the thinking project, all the ideas that you generated will be in one place (on the template) which acts as a convenient repository for your ideas on the topic for the future too.

It would be useful for you to have the templates to hand while you read this book so you become familiar with them and see how they can add benefit to your thinking. So why not print them out now before you start reading the next chapters on how to use the various toolsets?

Going solo or with a team

If you want to think about an issue on your own, then you can simply use the appropriate template to guide you through the project. However, in the business environment it's frequently useful (or necessary) to involve a number of other people. If you are the person who is setting up a team thinking project with a number of people, then Chapter 9 explains how to do this.

However, prior to you leading a team through a thinking project, it will be better to use the toolset yourself on a solo issue beforehand, so that you become familiar with the tool content and how the tools themselves actually work.

Some terminology

There are some words used throughout the explanation of the process that have a specifically relevant meaning and these are highlighted here.

- *Interrogate* is used frequently in the tools and this is an important concept. It relates to actively re-probing aspects of your business to find something new that has been missed before when any particular topic was considered in the past. And invariably there will be something that has been missed. The interrogation process may probe or question an issue from a number of different directions to prise out a valuable nugget of information. If you've ever noticed that many new ideas seem blindingly obvious in hindsight, it's probably because they were triggered by a previously unseen insight from a part of the business that people assumed was void of opportunity. Interrogating is effectively aimed at helping you to look at the same things that others previously looked at, but enabling you to see something different.

- *Templates* are the PDF documents that you can download and print out. They contain the structured approaches which act as a blueprint to lead you through your thinking project and are also the place where you capture all your ideas.

- *Toolsets* are the three different approaches that you can take depending on the category of thinking project you are undertaking: Islands of Opportunity; Divide and Conquer; and Boundary Riding. Each toolset contains five different thinking tools and includes an assessment and boosting section for your ideas at the end.

- *Tools* consist of individual frameworks and structured approaches, sometimes including a set of stimuli, that lead your thinking around a specifically focused element of your Killer Question. All the tools are different in format and in the way they lead your thinking.

- *Build/boost* relate to how an idea can be developed once it is identified. An idea, by default, is the first representation of a raw concept. When it is reviewed at the end of the toolset, there are always ways to build on it to make it more complete, or extend it to incorporate other related aspects. Similarly, it is usually possible to boost it in some way to take it further towards an end solution or to make it more comprehensive.

How the toolsets differ

- **Islands of Opportunity** is the initial toolset that you are most likely to use as it is designed to suit any type of issue. Once the Killer Question is defined, each of the five tools addresses the Killer Question as a single focus.

- **Divide and Conquer** commences by breaking the Killer Question down into a number of elements and separates them into those elements which have probably been considered previously in depth, and those that are potentially new areas of opportunity that may not have been given much attention. The toolset then focuses one tool on each of five of these new areas of opportunity.

- **Boundary Riding** is focused solely on the organic growth of your business. It looks at the opportunities that exist for you at the edges of your current realm of business in a number of different dimensions.

Throughout each of the toolsets are sections entitled Genius Spaces that look like this:

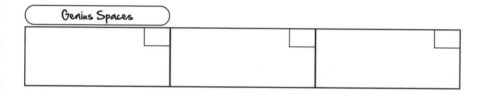

These are the places where you enter all your ideas. They are spread across the toolset to make it convenient for you, and you can enter your ideas in any of these spaces within a toolset. Only write one idea in each space and make sure you write sufficient detail so the idea will make sense to you later, when you return to review it. You don't have to fill all the Genius Spaces in – but the more you do complete, the better your potential solution is likely to be. You can ignore the small rectangle in each box for now – they are used later as part of the assessment process.

Now it's time to become The Idea Generator and to meet the toolsets themselves.

Islands of Opportunity (thinking tools 1–5)

Islands of Opportunity is a set of five tools to identify fresh opportunities and solutions for a new or existing issue that is being tackled for the first time. It's appropriate for most issues where there is a need to identify a wide range of possible answers to the Killer Question before selecting one ideal path forward to be developed. It's not intended for a difficult issue that has been considered many times before or where a number of new approaches are required for more complex issues. The second toolset (Divide and Conquer) is better suited for this purpose. Islands of Opportunity is an excellent introductory way to familiarise yourself with The Idea Generator approach and some of the tools and techniques used.

You can download the Islands of Opportunity template free of charge from: **www.TheIdeaGenerator.info**

Setting up your project

Has your Killer Question put you squarely in Querencia? If your question is open to being challenged then address those challenges before you start to answer it – don't try to justify your question to others through your answers. The more people that buy in and support your question before you answer it, then the deeper your question is sitting in Querencia.

Tool 1: Unconventional Perspectives

Considering an issue differently can be a difficult task to achieve, so this tool forces you to adopt a number of unusual viewpoints that may not have been applied before.

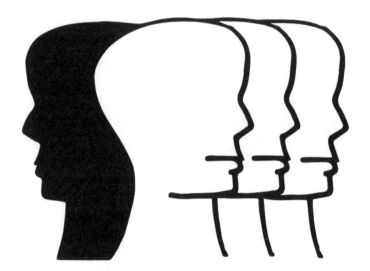

It's natural for you to approach any issue from the direction that you are most familiar with and which you know works well from your previous experience. However, this is likely to give you similar outcomes to those that you've had previously when faced with a new issue. To gain fresh insights, you need to consider the issue from a number of new and differentiated angles.

Unconventional Perspectives guides you to break the patterns of your usual approach and apply four alternative viewpoints instead to release new insights that would normally have been missed.

How the tool works

The four perspectives considered are:

- **Perspective 1: Is there a higher-level, more strategic issue that you should be considering instead?** What if you are just looking at a symptom and not the cause; or a side-effect that has distracted you from the central aspect? Or perhaps the source of the issue has been clouded from your sight in some way? What is this higher-level issue, and how would you address it?

- **Perspective 2: What would a ten-year-old child say was your real problem?** Would they cut to the chase and state the obvious to you even if it meant offending you? What are the obvious things that you are potentially overlooking?

- **Perspective 3: What unusual aspects of this issue would a leading expert recommend you focus on?** Are there some detailed elements that you are unaware of that could be critical? Where are the key leverage points to gain maximum benefit – and what should you do with these?

- **Perspective 4: What if you've made a big mistake and missed the point entirely – what else could it be?** Imagine that you've taken the wrong angle on this issue and got it completely the wrong way round. What might the real issue be?

For each of the four perspectives, write down a number of answers to the perspective questions posed. Then, consider each of these in turn to see what ideas can be identified from them. This is how the tool looks in the downloadable template:

Tool 1: Unconventional Perspectives

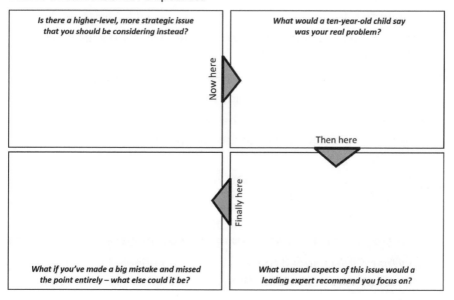

An example of the tool in use

If the example Killer Question is . . .

As a membership-based organisation, how do we attract more customers to join us?

. . . then some answers to the perspective questions that you'd enter in the appropriate boxes in the tool could be:

1 Is there a higher-level, more strategic issue that you should be considering instead?
   - Are we losing the new customers we acquire soon after they join? If so, what do we need to change to ensure they stay with us for longer?
   - Rather than have annual fees which require annual renewal, how can we change to perpetual weekly, monthly or quarterly fees?

2 What would a ten-year-old child say was your real problem?
   - Why don't you just get people to bring all their friends with them?
   - You want to make the people who aren't members of your gang jealous of the ones who have been allowed to be members.

3 What unusual aspects of this issue would a leading expert recommend you focus on?
   - Do you have proven insights from the minds of potential customers of how they decide on what to buy?
   - Show ways to create 'must have' membership offers for potential customers which are commercially viable for the business.

4 What if you've made a big mistake and missed the point entirely – what else could it be?
   - What if we only targeted 'large groups' of potential customers rather than focusing on individuals?
   - What if we changed to focus on getting people to be 'members for life' rather than being members for just a year?

You would now go back and review the above insights that have been identified through the four Unconventional Perspectives to see what ideas they trigger for you.

Some ideas from this example that you would write in your Genius Spaces are:

- Set up a round table approach with some other non-competing membership organisations/businesses to understand and share the best practices in ways to retain new members.
- Look at some alternative ways of charging members based on usage, participation, value added or taken away. Could fees change based on how 'profitable' customers are to the business – in the same way that insurance premiums are related to the claims made?
- How do we get people to bring their friends/circles/networks into being members in the same way that social networks enable people to be in different groups?
- Social networks have users – not members. Could we change our thinking to consider our customers as users instead of members?

Tips on using this tool

Don't always take the perspective literally when you apply it, as sometimes this may tend to constrain your thinking. Consider it in a broader context and let your mind make connections based on this breadth of connections. After all, it's the final ideas you are looking for, and whatever route you take to get them isn't important in the end – it's just the fact that you get the new ideas that matters.

Tool 2: Abstract. Move. Steal!

Rather than create something totally new from scratch, it's easier and quicker to take something that's already complete and that is proven to work in another area – and then steal it to use as a solution to your issue.

When looking for new ideas, it's natural to want to identify that amazing and truly original idea that's never been seen before, that will make you the hero of the moment for developing it. However, there are no truly original ideas. Not one. Because the way our mind works is that we take 'thought one' and combine it with 'thought two', to create a new 'thought three'. Now even though 'thought three' might seem to be a new idea, it's readily possible to see how it was created from earlier 'thought one' and 'thought two'. So rather than spend fruitless hours searching for a totally new idea, simply take an existing idea from elsewhere and modify it to suit your needs. This is about taking the easy option by stealing from elsewhere.

And to ensure you incorporate an essence of differentiation in the output, rather than steal your trigger idea from your competitors or from your own immediate industry, instead steal your idea from a completely different industry or business type.

How the tool works

Your Killer Question is intended to be highly specific to your particular issue – so the first stage is to raise your issue up to a more abstract level. This is a description that still encompasses what you desire to achieve but which at this more abstract level is also applicable elsewhere.

Abstracted
issue

Your
issue

You then need to move your abstracted issue sideways into different areas, so identify three industries that are completely unrelated to yours that also face this same, more abstracted issue.

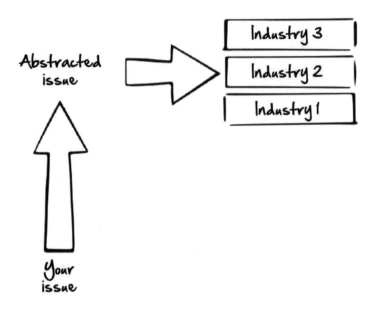

Now re-phrase your issue specifically to suit how each of these three industries would describe, or consider it.

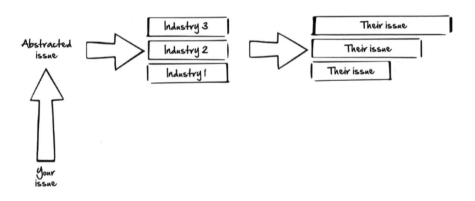

Next you must note some specific approaches in which each of these industries goes about addressing their version of your issue.

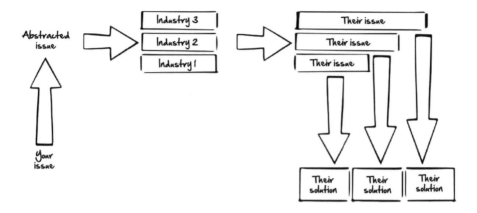

Then identify four ways in which each of the industries answers their version of your issue. These are called 'insight triggers' on the template.

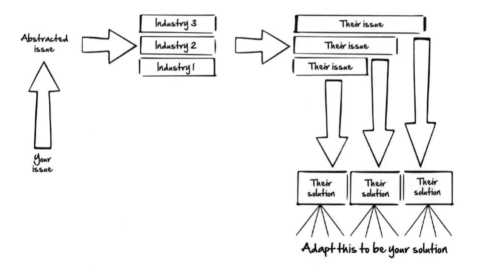

Adapt this to be your solution

Consider each of these insight triggers in turn and use them to form interesting connections that relate directly to your specific need. Identify some interesting ideas for each of these insight triggers that will help you answer your issue in some way.

Here's how the tool appears in the template:

Tool 2: Abstract. Move. Steal!

Your original issue

Your abstracted issue

Industry 1:

Their version of your issue:

Industry 2:

Their version of your issue:

Industry 3:

Their version of your issue:

What each of these industries actually does to address their version of your abstracted issues:

Insight triggers

-
-
-
-

Insight triggers

-
-
-
-

Insight triggers

-
-
-
-

An example of the tool in use

Imagine that your Killer Question is:

We are about to release a new version of our software product which we haven't updated for a long time. How do we get people to be aware of this update within a few weeks of launch?

The abstracted version of this Killer Question could be:

How does a fading entity get more attention rapidly?

You can abstract your issue in any number of different ways and it doesn't matter how you do it – just as long as you abstract it to make it a deliberately broad and generic issue. Now list three other industries that have this same abstracted issue – and note that we are using the term 'industries' in its widest possible sense to give us an expansive range of directions for our thinking. Let's assume the three industries chosen are music, film and household products.

An example of the abstracted question for each of these industries could be:

- **Music:** How do pop stars who have not had a hit song in some time make a come-back?
- **Film:** What do film stars do when they are no longer suitable for the roles that made them famous?
- **Household products:** How do you re-launch iconic products that have lost their lustre?

Now, look at what each of these industries does to get more attention, and then think how each of these principles could be applied to getting attention for your product's latest update.

Music: How do pop stars who have not had a hit song in some time make a come-back?

Examples from the music industry include releasing a new album that appeals to a different type of music lover; appearing on stage and having a 'wardrobe malfunction' to get press exposure; and giving free digital tracks away as part of a promotion.

The ideas these considerations might trigger for your software product include:

- Asking if the focus should be on getting the existing users to upgrade or whether greater value will be gained from appealing to new customers directly.
- Could it be launched as a new product to those who don't know of the old product?
- How could people who are willing to 'expose themselves' as users of the old product be given a new version as a trial?

Film: What do film stars do when they are no longer suitable for the roles that made them famous?

Examples are to start directing or producing films; be the big-named star in alternative or independent films; and move on to doing advertisements for products.

The ideas these considerations might trigger for your software product include:

- Is there value in downgrading the appeal of the product from an optional high-end choice to becoming a must-have utility or commodity item?
- Is there a way to get new appeal to the long-serving customers of the older product to act as the 'voice of long experience' to attract new customers?
- How can being an old established product be of value in a marketplace being constantly flooded by newcomers – who you know won't last long?

Household products: How do you re-launch iconic products that have lost their lustre?

Examples include Marmite and their love-it-or-hate-it campaign; and Wispa, the Cadbury's chocolate bar that was revived due to an online campaign by former lovers of the product.

The ideas these considerations might trigger for your software product include:

- What are some ways to get people to refrain from being un-committal to your product and be confident that the product is either definitely for them – or not for them? This will help to focus your efforts on who to target.
- Can you engage with all the existing users to find out what they'd want in an upgrade – and then tell them that the new version will incorporate some of their desired features?

Tips on using this tool

Recognise that nothing is ever truly new and original, and that your issue has almost certainly been addressed before in another industry or situation. It may appear in a disguised or alternative form, so look closely at what's being done elsewhere – and learn from it for your own purpose.

Tool 3: Rapid Thinking

A technique that drives you to think quickly and capture lots of ideas around an issue to prevent you filtering and rejecting ideas due to the personal internal thinking style you usually apply.

Some people have the knack of being able to spew out ideas whenever they are needed, whereas others find this almost impossible. The ones who find it difficult to achieve this generally do so because they are putting internal filters in their minds and trying to create an idea and evaluate it at the same time. Creating and evaluating are two very different cognitive processes and if you try to do both in parallel you will get stuck between the two. Your creativity will suffer and the evaluation side of your thinking will end up rejecting everything – which starts a reinforcing loop in your mind that you can't generate creative ideas.

Another reason is that people fear failure and so don't want to suggest ideas that are less than great. However, if you try to avoid failure, you'll fail to generate ideas and will subsequently fail to find success. Remember that of all the ideas you develop, when you evaluate them later, the vast majority won't make it past the first stage of assessment. It's not necessarily that they were bad ideas; they just weren't as good (appropriate, targeted, relevant etc.) as the ideas that were chosen to go forward to the next stage.

Some of your output will be half-formed or ambiguous and while it may not appear to make sense during the 'bulk-splurging' phase of idea generation, when you consider it afterwards you'll see where it came from and how it has better potential if modified or re-written.

How the tool works

The aim of this tool is to burst through your initial considerations of where success may lie by minimising qualitative limitations to your thinking through the application of time pressure. A tight time limit of five minutes is imposed to deliver 30 ideas to complete the Rapid Thinking framework. That's one idea every ten seconds.

You initially think of approximately 12 potential areas of your core issue where interesting ideas might arise from. These could be from different components of the issue, features, customer types, process elements, departments or areas that may form a core part of a solution – or any other specific or interesting aspect of the issue. Then you select the five most opportune areas to consider. The five you choose could be a mix of any of these suggestions – or they may be five variations around the same theme. Once you've identified the five interesting areas, write one in each of the five tool segments – as indicated below.

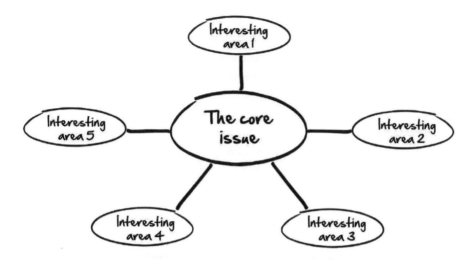

When you've entered the five interesting areas you will focus on, you can then proceed to complete the tool. For each of these five focus areas, you are going to aim to identify three conventional ideas for that focus and also three unconventional ideas. This is indicated on the diagram below:

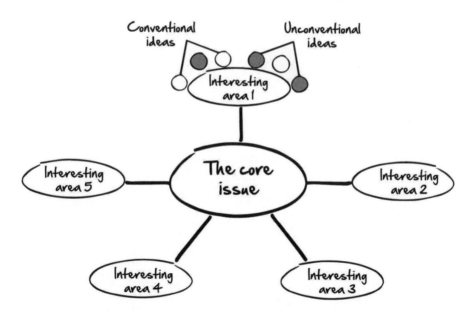

Once the tool is prepared, set the timer on your watch or phone and give yourself five minutes to fill in the 30 empty blocks for the conventional and unconventional thoughts with an idea that relates to your focus area – and which of course is aimed at addressing your Killer Question.

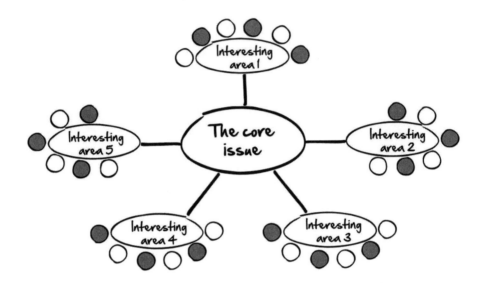

Here's how the tool looks in the template.

Tool 3: Rapid Thinking

Potential interesting areas to consider (12 needed)

	Conventional ideas	Unconventional ideas
Interesting area 1		
Interesting area 2		
Interesting area 3		
Interesting area 4		
Interesting area 5		

Once the framework is complete, you can then review all the ideas you have generated. Because you've come up with these ideas at speed, they may be a little lacking in clarity and direction, so you need to select some of them to be developed further. Identify the four that (in your personal opinion) are the most interesting or that have the greatest potential, and copy them into the four Idea Booster ovals. Then spend a few minutes boosting each of these four selected ideas by reviewing and developing them in several different directions so they are more meaningful and valuable. Capture your useful ideas in the Genius Spaces. Part of the Rapid Thinking Idea Booster tool is shown here:

Tool 3: Rapid Thinking – Idea Boosters

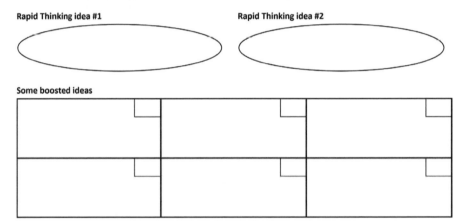

Rapid Thinking idea #1

Rapid Thinking idea #2

Some boosted ideas

An example of the tool in use

Let's assume that your example issue is:

How can we get the skilled people we need to want to move to the rural part of the country where our company is based?

Some of the interesting areas that you could consider for this issue are:

- Locality – show the benefits of the area
- Remuneration – different ways of paying and rewarding employees

- Lifestyle – demonstrate better lifestyle options
- Work – explain the interesting aspects of the role
- Financial – what the financial benefits of moving to the area are
- Family – the options for children and family in the area

There could be many different ways of breaking the issue down into interesting areas to consider – you could have focused entirely on the aspects of your business, for example. Once you've entered your five selected interesting areas into the five boxes in the Rapid Thinking framework, you then start the clock and think fast for five minutes to complete the framework. A completed part of the framework for the example issue is shown below.

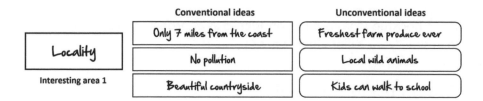

Because these ideas were generated at speed they may be lacking a little in quality – so while everything that you've written is still fresh in your mind, review all your ideas and copy the five most interesting ones into the Idea Booster ovals. You will now enhance some of your original ideas to boost them into something more powerful. A part of the Idea Booster is shown below.

Tool 3: Rapid Thinking — Idea Boosters

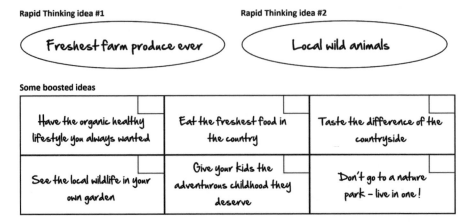

Rapid Thinking idea #1

Freshest farm produce ever

Rapid Thinking idea #2

Local wild animals

Some boosted ideas

Have the organic healthy lifestyle you always wanted	Eat the freshest food in the country	Taste the difference of the countryside
See the local wildlife in your own garden	Give your kids the adventurous childhood they deserve	Don't go to a nature park – live in one!

These boosted ideas can be considered as approaches that can help you to answer your Killer Question.

Tips on using this tool

To prevent yourself from starting to self-censor your ideas, be focused on completing the required number of ideas (no matter how extreme) within the specified time. This is purely about quantity over quality, as the quality will come from the ideas you take forward for boosting. Resist the internal censoring urge and just keep writing.

Many of the people who can splurge ideas in the moment know that there's a lot of uncertainty and vagueness related to their creative output – but they have confidence in themselves that in amongst the quantity, are some practical and good quality ideas. And frequently one decent idea is all that is required. So have confidence in your mental abilities – after all, you are a reasonably bright person, aren't you?

Continued experience in using this Rapid Thinking approach to generate ideas will build your confidence and develop your quick-thinking abilities.

Tool 4: DARPEC

An approach to help you understand how every interaction has six generic aspects and to force you to de-construct the issue you are facing and focus on each of these aspects individually.

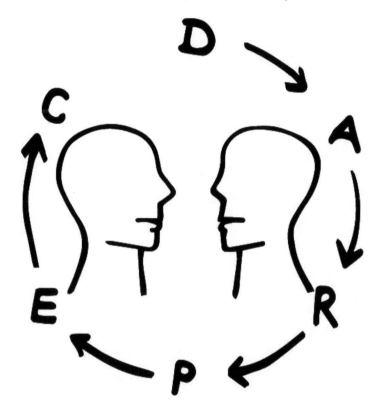

We frequently try to focus on the 'core' of any interaction to see how it can be improved. However, there are more aspects that relate to the core activity and that can have an impact on it in different ways than we may normally consider. This tool helps us to consider all aspects of an interaction.

How the tool works

DARPEC is an acronym for any generic interaction that we perform in the business environment. It stands for a *Deliverer* performs an *Action* for the benefit of a *Recipient* using a *Process* in an *Environment* under certain *Constraints*. Its aim is to help you look differently and in detail at the activities occurring that are related to your issue. For each of the six elements of the DARPEC model, there is a series of questions posed that helps you to interrogate your issue in more detail and so identify solutions or opportunities that may be of great value.

DELIVERER

- What is the ideal goal of the deliverer?
- How can this be achieved more readily?
- What prevents them from doing this perfectly?
- Is this aligned to what the recipient wants?

ACTION

- What is the process being undertaken?
- How could it be more effective?
- Who is the best party to help this happen quicker?
- Where might this be changed for the better?

RECIPIENT

- What is the ideal outcome for the recipient?
- Why is this not being achieved currently?
- How could this be an amazing experience for the recipient?
- Who else could benefit from this transaction?

PROCESS

- Which elements of this process seem wasteful or out-dated?
- Who is involved in the process, and are they the best people for it?
- What's the core activity of what needs to happen here?

ENVIRONMENT

- How could the environment be more conducive to the process?
- What's wrong with the environment now?
- How can it be better for the parties involved?

CONSTRAINTS

- What are the limiting constraints on this action?
- How can they be relaxed to make it easier for this to happen?
- Where could you apply constraints that would ensure this activity happens more efficiently?

Here's how the Deliverer part of the DARPEC tool appears in the template:

Tool 4: DARPEC

DELIVERER
- What is the ideal goal of the deliverer?
- How can this be achieved more readily?
- What prevents them from doing this perfectly?
- Is this aligned to what the recipient wants?

What's the **DELIVERER's** situation?

Consider each of these questions in turn and answer them such that your answers could improve the issue in your Killer Question.

An example of the tool in use

If your issue is:

How can we provide better customer service through our contact centres when handling customer complaints in order to lift our customer satisfaction scores in the next six months?

Going through each element sequentially, we can identify opportunities that are triggered by our understanding of this specific aspect of the interaction:

Deliverer: The deliverer will usually be the employee on the end of the phone, but it may also extend to the rest of the service team and to anyone else who may be involved in resolving the customer's complaint.

- Run a 30-day trial with one team to remove all their productivity measures and allow them to take as long as is necessary to resolve a customer's query.
- As our products are batch-manufactured, always inform the advisors immediately if there appears to be any problem at all with a specific product batch – along with recommended courses of action.
- At random, have a senior executive make a follow-up phone call to the customer to ensure they are completely satisfied with the outcome. This is also a great PR opportunity too.

Action: The employee is trying to answer the customer's questions but might not be aware of the full story behind the complaint and so may be unable to perform as well as they'd ideally like to.

- Ensure all service advisors have a single view of the customer's relationship with us on their computer screen when talking to a customer.
- Every morning have a five-minute update for staff on their screens of new marketing collateral that has been issued in the last 24 hours to ensure they are up to speed on anything a customer may call in about.
- Open a conversation with an apology and offer to help the customer but use the brief time while their details are being called up to ask how their day is going to pick up what frame of mind they are in – so you can respond accordingly.

Recipient: This is the customer who has called in to the contact centre who may be completely right in what they are saying – or they may be completely wrong. Also, the customer is only human and may have made a mistake. This won't be known until the issue is resolved – and even then the personality of the customer may be a difficult one to satisfy.

- Always offer to send the customer an email notification or transcript of the call to remind them of the outcome once the issue is rectified, as many calls are made by customers while they are on the move so they can't write things down.
- Sometimes elderly customers are just wanting someone to talk to – so is there an option to pass the call on to an elderly advisor who knows how to handle these calls and is employed specifically for this purpose to free up the higher-trained advisors for other calls?

- Have the mindset that the client is a famous celebrity and has a million followers on Twitter that they have the potential to tweet to about the service you deliver.

Process: The employee is probably following a process dictated by the system they are using in their effort to help the customer, but the customer also has an expectation of a process of 'how this call should go' in their mind.

- Ensure every call that takes longer than ten minutes to resolve is highlighted for a root-cause analysis by the productivity team to remedy problem issues at the source.
- Empower employees to immediately reimburse business customers with a product refund voucher up to a value of £100 where it appears our product is at fault.
- Encourage the customer to give feedback on the effectiveness of the resolution by telling them how it's part of an improvement programme to prevent future occurrences of their complaint. Assess how the advisors with the best scores are interacting so successfully with the customers and share these learnings.

Environment: The medium is a phone call where many aspects of the interaction can't be shared, such as human emotion and even physical items. But while the employee may be seated in their purposefully designed contact centre, the customer may be trying to do this while they are at work, while on public transport, while minding children or in any number of other inconvenient environments.

- Arrange for some home-based advisors to be available for intermittent periods during the day when we have peak volumes, e.g. at lunchtime and evening commuting time.
- Allow the advisor to share a webcam video of themselves while they are resolving the customer's issue to help deepen the personal side of the activity while the call is in progress.
- Invite the areas of the business who are responsible for the root cause of the complaint to sit in on calls for a few hours to fully understand the issues the customer is having with the part of the overall proposition they are responsible for.

Constraints: Both the employee and the customer may not have all the information needed to help each other. Additionally, the customer may be under time constraints – especially if the transaction starts to take a prolonged period of time to resolve.

- Offer to call the customer back at a more convenient time for them – which allows us to schedule calls and staff up accordingly.
- Use predictive analytics of previous calls on this same subject to advise the customer approximately how long the resolution will take – and offer to talk to them at a more convenient time if it will be too long for them now.
- Rather than being viewed as a major problem, complaints can be considered as gifts to us – tremendous opportunities to demonstrate how great we are as a company at fixing things when they go astray. So we should have this attitude when handling the complaints.

All these issues – from both sides of the transaction – need to be considered in order to identify opportunities for improvement in the Killer Question posed.

Tips on using this tool

Consider the full implications of what's going on both directly and indirectly in relation to any particular interaction to understand where some interesting detail exists that could be the source of new inspiration around the issue. The devil may be in the detail – but often the opportunities are too.

Tool 5: The Magnifying Matrix

This helps you to focus closely on specific combinations of aspects of your issue that you may not have previously considered or been aware of.

One of the attributes discussed when we looked at The Idea Generator mindset was the ability to make new connections that trigger new ideas. The Magnifying Matrix forces connections to be made between a number of your products or services and some of your key capabilities. This is achieved through the use of a matrix which enables you to gain new insights by 'force matching' things that may not have been considered together before.

How the tool works

Select four of your main business products or services that represent a diverse range of your propositions to customers. These will form the contents of the left side of the matrix.

Then identify four of the capabilities that your business excels at. In the same manner as you did with the products and services, aim to select a broad and varied range of your capabilities. These may include facets that you are rated highly on by customers, or that are critical in nature for you as a business, or they may represent some strategic asset that you have, such as a partner or location.

Specific examples of capabilities may include your support service, your on-site installation teams, a key distribution partner that you have or the fact that you are the only one among your competitors to have city-centre located facilities. These capabilities form the contents of the top row of your matrix. Your matrix can then be created as follows:

	Capability #1	Capability #2	Capability #3	Capability #4
Product or service #1				
Product or service #2				
Product or service #3				
Product or service #4				

You don't have to consider every combination of products or services with the corresponding capability, as some obvious pairings that the business may have considered before can be crossed out. An example of this may be where your on-site support (Capability #2) that you provide for your ABC proposition (Product #3) has won awards and is one of the flagship achievements that you talk about frequently in your marketing. You may wish to ignore this as potentially there isn't much room for improvement in this specific area, while there are other areas which form quite unusual combinations that are worthy of your thinking effort.

An example of the tool in use

Imagine that you are a product manufacturer selling tools and equipment through retail outlets to consumers for emergencies in the home. You are looking for ways to gain a greater awareness of your products. The various products and services you sell and the key capabilities you have may include the following:

PRODUCTS/SERVICES	KEY CAPABILITIES
Household safety items and equipment	An approved safety supplies manufacturer
Emergency back-up items	Wide range of 'how to' videos available
Essential car supplies for an emergency	You employ female demonstrators
Personal protective devices	Long established in your industry

This allows you to create your Magnifying Matrix as follows:

You may decide that the first matrix box where 'safety items' intersects with 'approved manufacturer' doesn't offer much opportunity as it's a given expectation by customers that any good quality safety equipment would, by default, need to be made by an approved manufacturer. So you could put a cross in this box and ignore it.

However, the next matrix intersection to the right (where 'safety items' intersects with 'many "how to" videos') offers a great marketing and

PR opportunity to educate people how to do what many people may regard as potentially risky tasks safely, if they use the correct (your) safety equipment. This would be a great series of videos to upload to your own branded YouTube channel to support customers and also to appeal to potential customers too.

Similarly for the next intersection to the right. It would be a powerful way to demonstrate to potential female customers, who may feel they can't do certain tasks around the home, that women are equally as capable as men by showing your female demonstrators using your equipment to complete a wide range of tasks easily and safely.

By running through all the intersections on the matrix, you will experience forced connections that you wouldn't normally make if you hadn't been using the Magnifying Matrix tool. All the ideas that you identify from using the tool should be entered into your Genius Spaces.

Tips on using this tool

Avoid choosing four variations of the same product range or four variations of similar capabilities that you have. Aim to get a diverse selection for each part of the matrix. Also try randomly jumping around the matrix using two different products/services and capabilities each time rather that moving along a row or down a column in an orderly manner. This helps to break the thinking pattern you had associated with one product or capability by switching your thinking into another area each time.

Assessment and building stage

At this point you have completed the creative part of your thinking project and now need to assess your captured output and build on the best thoughts to turn them into winning ideas.

In the Genius Spaces where you've been writing all your ideas, there's a small rectangle in the top-right corner which you'll use for the initial selection of your best ideas. You should now review all your ideas and select the 20 that you think are the most interesting, or which have the greatest potential in the way they might answer your Killer Question. You can write the letters 'A' to 'T' in these small rectangles for the ideas that you select. An example of this is shown below.

This isn't a ranking of any kind – it's simply a process to identify the top ideas to carry forward. If the number of ideas you select is slightly more or less than 20, then this is okay – just use the appropriate number of letters of the alphabet. Twenty is just a target to aim for so you don't end up selecting too few or too many ideas. When you've selected your best ideas you then proceed to plot them on the Impact–Implementation Grid. An example of a blank Impact–Implementation Grid is shown below.

Islands of Opportunity: Impact – Implementation Grid

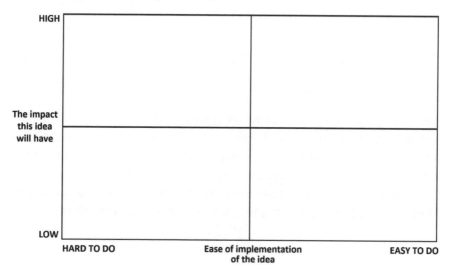

The vertical axis on the left is the size of the impact that this idea will have on answering the Killer Question. The higher the impact the idea will have, the higher up the grid the idea will be positioned. The horizontal axis is the ease of implementation of the idea. If it will be hard to implement then it goes towards the left side of the grid and if it is relatively easy to implement, it will be positioned towards the right side of the grid.

The aim is to now position all of your 'A' to 'T' lettered ideas onto the Impact–Implementation Grid. The letters you have allocated can be used to identify the location of the idea on the grid. (The letters are more convenient to use than having to re-write the whole idea out.) An example of a partially completed grid is shown below.

Islands of Opportunity: Impact – Implementation Grid

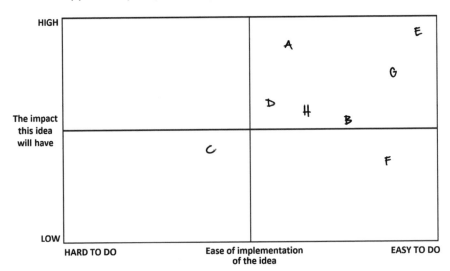

Once all your identified ideas are positioned on the grid, it's easy to see which ones should be taken forward. The ones that are located towards the top-right corner are those that will have the biggest impact on the Killer Question and which are also the easier ones to implement. The ones in the lower-left quadrant should be avoided as these have a lower impact and are also harder to implement.

You now want to select your top four ideas (in order) and copy their description into the spaces in the Building Blocks. Start with the idea that is located in the most upper-right position on the Impact–Implementation Grid and copy this into the #1 idea position. Then copy the next most upper-right positioned idea into the #2 idea position, and similarly for the next two ideas in order. A blank example is shown below.

Islands of Opportunity: Building Blocks

Your #1 idea

Relevant matters	Ways to build this idea

For each of the four selected ideas note down some relevant facts or additional thoughts that will build on this initial idea and potentially convert it into a winning idea. Imagine that the most upper-right idea from the Impact–Implementation Grid is to offer industry best practice delivery times for online orders, and you enter this in the first position in the Building Blocks.

Now, you may be aware of some information that could be relevant in enhancing this idea such as the fact that your company is looking for ways to offer a premium range of services to customers, your contract with your current delivery company is coming up for renegotiation soon, and that one of your competitors already offers much better delivery times than you do.

These can be noted down in the 'relevant matters' area of the idea's Building Blocks. Then you can use these combinations of knowledge to stimulate further thinking and form new mental connections to create a boosted version of your idea. This becomes the new version of your original idea. A completed Building Blocks example is shown below.

Islands of Opportunity: Building Blocks

Your #1 idea

> Offer industry best practice delivery times for online orders

Relevant matters	Ways to build this idea
We want to offer a premium service.	See if a new delivery partner can offer a next-day delivery service.
Our annual delivery contract is due for renewal soon.	Get the contracts department on-board with this idea before they start negotiations.
Competitor XYZ offers better delivery.	

Your #2 idea

> Help customers by un-crating products and removing the packaging

Relevant matters	Ways to build this idea
Good environmental aspect.	Get people to commit by booking the service in advance.
It can be a premium service offer that we can charge extra for.	Allows the delivery people to engage with their staff – and we can use this time to find out more about their business and needs.

Positioning your ideas for success

If you are working on this project alone, then these ideas become your output and you shape them into the solution you will either use, or present to other people for buy-in and approval. If you are doing this project as part of a team exercise then when you have to present your idea, offer it as a suggested 'starter idea' for consideration by the others involved. Avoid trying to position it as the definitive solution to the world's problems. You want to win people over to your idea and your way of thinking – and the best way to achieve this is to let them decide they want your idea to go forward and that they want to be part of it too. You may not realise that your idea is actually an offer – where you invite others to join onto your idea, and you encourage them to build it up with their own ideas – just as you use your stock of ideas to help build up other's ideas too.

If you've been invited to form part of a facilitated Synergising Session (discussed in Chapter 9), then the leader will ask each person to offer their best idea in turn and then to cycle round all participants in layers, with each person offering their second, third, and finally fourth idea until all the participant's ideas have been explained. Then will come the exercise of combining and synergising all the ideas into one or more preferred and agreed ways forward.

Here are some tips for ensuring your ideas are seen as winning ideas:

- Don't try to over-sell your ideas but instead try to present them so others feel they are the natural ways forward. This helps you get buy-in from others based on the quality and clarity of your ideas.
- In this regard, make sure your idea is presented clearly so all understand it immediately. While it may be clear to you, it may not be clear to others.
- Getting the high-level principle written down on a sticky-note is a good exercise in making it succinct in just a few words.
- Write it neatly so everyone can read it without effort, and try to make it stand out on a flipchart in some way.
- Don't aim to go for a 'finalised end solution' – instead go for a starting point that others can build on. This will stimulate others to have their own reason to be on-board with it as they can incorporate some of their own thinking to it. Present your ideas as triggers for further development rather than absolute solutions.

You may like to imagine how wonderful it would be if you were celebrated as the identifier of the ultimate solution to an issue. Unfortunately, the chance of this happening is very slim, as your idea will probably be adapted many times on its journey to execution. So recognise this, and instead be the person who starts the thinking along a specific direction with your winning idea. You may consider that you'll lose some of the glory but the aim is to help the business achieve its goal, not necessarily to celebrate individual heroes.

What will potentially happen is that people will recognise you as the one who is good at identifying the route that should be taken towards the desired goal. Subsequently you may find that your skills as The Idea Generator will be in demand in different areas of the business. And that's not a bad business to be in!

Divide and Conquer (thinking tools 6–10)

Divide and Conquer is a set of five tools to address a difficult issue or an issue that has been scrutinised previously but without any meaningful success, and where some new ideas are needed. If the Islands of Opportunity toolset was used, it may end up covering the same ground as before, and so this toolset helps to leapfrog over the areas that have (most likely) already been covered to identify and interrogate new areas that have potential for success.

The Divide and Conquer toolset template can be downloaded for free from: **www.TheIdeaGenerator.info**

Setting up your project

You start by phrasing your Killer Question in the same manner as explained previously. Again, ensure that once you've created it, it meets the requirements of a great Killer Question and puts you firmly into Querencia.

Then think about broad areas where a solution might lie. Consider the areas or aspects of the issue where you suspect people may have looked for a solution in the past – and create a list of them with the title EXHAUSTED areas. Aim to make this list at least ten items long. Follow this with a second list entitled CHALLENGING areas. Under this heading identify some unusual, interesting, off-beat or edgy areas where a solution might be found. You aren't trying to identify the actual solution here – just some non-conventional and differentiated areas where a solution or opportunity might exist. This list should be between eight and ten items long.

As an example, imagine that your Killer Question was:

How do we get more people to serve themselves online instead of visiting a branch or calling up our contact centre?

Then you may make the following lists of EXHAUSTED and CHALLENGING areas:

EXHAUSTED AREAS	CHALLENGING AREAS
TV and radio adverts	Helping people to learn a skill
Mailshots	Rewarding people who self-serve
Limiting availability of hours	Being self-sufficient
Hiding the necessary information	Saving time by serving yourself
Emails with information links	Specific benefits per customer type
Signage in the branches	Make it the smart thing to do
In-branch giveaways	Making it really interesting
Internet advertising	Make it a talking point in social media
YouTube videos	Educate people in some way
Tweeting information	Having new features to give it appeal

Highlight the five CHALLENGING areas that you believe may offer the greatest potential for success in answering your Killer Question and identify them 'A' to 'E' in any order. You will use the CHALLENGING area marked as 'A' with the first tool in this section (Tool 6), the one marked 'B' with the second tool in this section (Tool 7) and so on for all five CHALLENGING areas and tools.

For each tool you will probably need to amend your Killer Question slightly so that it aligns with the area you've identified for that tool. This approach helps you to 'leapfrog' over the EXHAUSTED areas which have a high probability of having been unsuccessfully covered before, and to apply your thinking energy through The Idea Generator on the CHALLENGING and potentially new areas for exploration.

Continuing with the example, if you chose 'Rewarding people who self-serve' from the above list as your CHALLENGING area 'A', then you may amend your Killer Question for the first tool to be:

How could we reward people for using online self-serve instead of visiting a branch or calling up the contact centre?

If you chose 'Saving time by serving yourself' as your CHALLENGING area 'B', then you may similarly amend your Killer Question for the second tool to be:

How do we encourage huge numbers of people to serve themselves online by showing them how much time they will all save?

Modifying the Killer Question this way helps to keep it aligned to your high-level goal while also allowing you to explore multiple interesting focus areas rather than considering just one area.

Tool 6: All Change Please!

Frequently, our thinking is caged by a set of beliefs or assumptions that we believe to be fixed. This tool helps to question the core assumptions being made around the selected CHALLENGING area.

Sometimes in life you take things for granted and assume that they can't be changed. These assumptions then begin to form a series of constraints to your thinking which limits your options for success. This tool tests these assumptions to see where they can be changed, relaxed, or even eliminated, to give you greater freedom for thinking and to discover fresh opportunities.

How the tool works

From the project set-up, take your CHALLENGING area 'A' and re-write your Killer Question to incorporate this area. The tool then guides you through a list of interrogators to reconsider the different types of assumptions you are making around your Killer Question. For each of the Who?, What?, When?, Where?, Why? and How? aspects of the issue, you must list the relevant assumptions you are making – and then check whether they are truly valid assumptions.

The 'Who?' assumptions:

- Who is responsible for the outcome?
- Who is supposed to take the action?
- Who makes the key decision?
- Who is being missed out?
- Who is this aimed at?
- Who are the correct target audience?
- Who else should be included or excluded?

The 'What?' assumptions:

- What is the essential component of this?
- What constrains this from being much more effective/better?
- What is the key success measure in place?
- What if this measure was different?
- What timeframe defines the process?
- What is influencing the environment in which it occurs?

The 'When?' assumptions:

- When in the process does this take place?
- When are people ready to do this?
- When is the action deemed to be complete?
- When do the cycles start and finish?

- When is the most critical activity happening?
- When would people prefer to do this?

The 'Where?' assumptions:

- Where does this have to happen?
- Where are the key players at the time?
- Where is the key decision made?
- Where are the support mechanisms for this?
- Where is an ideal place for this?

The 'Why?' assumptions:

- Why are people involved at the points they currently are?
- Why is it this way?
- Why is it so complicated?
- Why would it be better done somewhere else?
- Why does this have to happen at all?
- Why are we (only) involved here?

The 'How?' assumptions:

- How does each stage add value?
- How do the participants feel during the process?
- How is this secure?
- How did this get to be so complicated?
- How could this be done quicker?
- How would things differ if we stopped it altogether?

Once you've noted all the assumptions you are making, you then review these to see which can be changed, reversed, relaxed, amended in some way – or even eliminated completely. With these revised assumptions in place you can then explore for how these changes may offer opportunity with regard to your CHALLENGING area under consideration, and enter these ideas in your Genius Spaces.

Here's how the tool looks in the templates:

Tool 6: All Change Please!

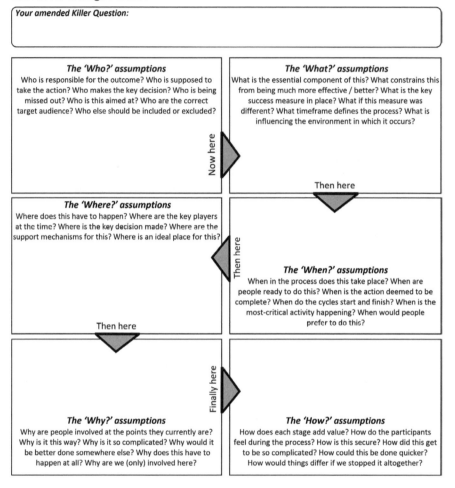

Your amended Killer Question:

The 'Who?' assumptions
Who is responsible for the outcome? Who is supposed to take the action? Who makes the key decision? Who is being missed out? Who is this aimed at? Who are the correct target audience? Who else should be included or excluded?

Now here →

The 'What?' assumptions
What is the essential component of this? What constrains this from being much more effective / better? What is the key success measure in place? What if this measure was different? What timeframe defines the process? What is influencing the environment in which it occurs?

Then here

The 'Where?' assumptions
Where does this have to happen? Where are the key players at the time? Where is the key decision made? Where are the support mechanisms for this? Where is an ideal place for this?

Then here

The 'When?' assumptions
When in the process does this take place? When are people ready to do this? When is the action deemed to be complete? When do the cycles start and finish? When is the most-critical activity happening? When would people prefer to do this?

Then here

Finally here →

The 'Why?' assumptions
Why are people involved at the points they currently are? Why is it this way? Why is it so complicated? Why would it be better done somewhere else? Why does this have to happen at all? Why are we (only) involved here?

The 'How?' assumptions
How does each stage add value? How do the participants feel during the process? How is this secure? How did this get to be so complicated? How could this be done quicker? How would things differ if we stopped it altogether?

An example of the tool in use

Imagine that your example CHALLENGING element as reflected by your re-worded Killer Question is:

How can we speed up our customers' finance application process?

From the various interrogators listed, you can identify the assumptions that can be tested – and the ways in which they can be pragmatically changed. Here are examples for some of the interrogation areas:

The assumption is: 'The process takes 48 hours to approve.'

The changes that can be proposed:

- How to reduce this to 24 hours/same working day/within one hour?
- What takes up these 48 hours? Is it sitting in a pile somewhere?
- Is anything being done on the application overnight? If not, why not?

The assumption is: 'The document has to go through all the various departments in sequence.'

The changes that can be proposed:

- What if one person from each department were in a room together and they passed it on as soon as their part was done? How quickly could the application be approved then?
- What if the various departments were replaced by one combined approvals team?

The assumption is: 'Physical documents have to be supplied with the application.'

The changes that can be proposed:

- How can certified digital copies be used more efficiently?
- Is it possible to access these key documents from the source database if the applicant gives their permission?

The assumption is: 'The customer is informed of the outcome by the credit control team.'

The changes that can be proposed:

- Let the introducer who met the customer inform them of their application result to deepen the personal relationship.

- Encourage a re-submission if the application failed on a minor point rather than a formal, finalised rejection.

Completing this tool

On the template for this tool, in the Genius Spaces where you've been writing your ideas, there is a small rectangle in the top-right corner. You need to mark all the ideas you've written down for this tool with the notation 'A' as shown below. This indicates that this idea relates to CHALLENGING area 'A'.

You will do a similar exercise at the end of each of the other tools in this toolset using the notation 'B' for the Tool 7 ideas, 'C' for Tool 8 ideas, and so on.

Tips on using this tool

There will be many assumptions which you are making which are totally valid and which it is impractical to try to challenge as they perform a useful or essential purpose – so accept these after due consideration. However, it only takes one or two assumptions that can be changed to offer significant opportunity for benefit.

Tool 7: Different People. Different Worlds

Looking at how another established industry that is significantly different to yours considers the issue you have, can help you break your patterns of thinking.

In many situations it makes sense to consider how any issue is being handled by competitors within your industry to see what can be learned from them. Even just adopting your industry's best practice may yield numerous opportunities for you. However, there's probably a good chance these things have been considered (and even tried) before, and if the issue still exists then you need to contemplate something distinctly different. This tool will help you achieve this.

How the tool works

The template contains a large selection of people in different professions to yours who work in other worlds (industries), and you need to select one at random from the supplied list. Here's an extract from the tool in the template:

Tool 7: Different People. Different Worlds.

Talk radio host	Physical therapist	Chinese restaurant owner	Interpreter	Spy	Pharmacist
Farmer	Deep-sea fisherman	Carpenter	Lawyer	Chiropodist	Accountant	Sea captain
Firefighter	Librarian	Astronomer	Sound engineer	Surveyor	Comedian	Pilot	Surgeon
Primary school teacher	Optometrist	The Pope	Hairdresser	Judge	Dentist	Nurse
Blacksmith	Architect	Body builder	Economist	Bank robber	Engineer	Tattoo artist
Policeman	Special forces soldier	Racing car driver	Social worker	Air traffic controller
Psychologist	Journalist	Hotel receptionist	Vet	Balloon-animal maker	Cartoonist
Sommelier	Botanist	Poet	Software programmer	Immunologist	Acupuncturist	Actuary

Select one of these different worlds at random. Then take your CHALLENGING area 'B' and re-write your Killer Question to match this world. You need to consider your issue from the perspective of this industry and the professionals who work in it, and it may be necessary to abstract your issue slightly to make it relevant. For example, if your issue was related to perishable products (for example, fresh fruit) you may abstract this to relate to items with a short shelf life (your fruit goes off quickly) or items that need to be kept in a controlled (chilled) environment or items that are delicate (fruit bruises easily).

Once you've abstracted your issue, you can then apply a number of interrogation questions to understand how your selected different world might handle the situation. The questions to use are:

1 What's an equivalent situation or analogous scenario in the different world to the issue that you have?
2 List some ways in which they address this issue in the different world. How can you interpret these to be relevant to your issue?
3 What are some specific measures the different world applies? How can you use these principles for your issue?
4 If a professional from this industry were to take control of your area, what changes would they make to address your issue from their expertise perspective?
5 What is something unusual or unique to this different world in regard to how they handle their version of your issue? How can this be applied to your benefit?

From here, you relate these insights to your issue and note down the ideas that arise from them. Here's the tool as it appears in the template:

Tool 7: Different People. Different Worlds.

Your amended Killer Question:

1) What's an equivalent situation or analogous scenario in the different world to the issue that you have?

"   "

2) List some ways in which they address this issue in the different world. How can you interpret these to be relevant to your issue?

"   "

- •   •
- •   •

3) What are some specific measures the different world applies? How can you use these principles for your issue?

"   "

- •   •
- •   •

4) If a professional from this industry were to take control of your area, what changes would they make to address your issue from their expertise perspective?

"   "

- •   •
- •   •

5) What is something unusual or unique to this different world in regard to how they handle their version of your issue? How can this be applied to your benefit?

"   "

- •   •
- •   •

An example of the tool in use

Assume the different professional that is randomly chosen is the 'talk radio' host and your amended Killer Question relevant to your challenging element is:

How can we instil confidence in our customers that their personal information is secure with us?

We can then pose the five interrogation questions to this issue:

1 What's an equivalent situation or analogous scenario in the different world to the issue that you have?

'How does the 'talk radio' industry get people to listen to, trust and enjoy the various show hosts?'

2 List some ways in which they address this issue in the different world. How can you interpret these to be relevant to your issue?

'They put the shows on at scheduled times so people know when they can hear their favourite presenter. The shows are named after the host. The hosts are seen to be public figures interacting with their listeners by social media, email, text and phone. They have a theme such as sport, news or general chat topics.'

Triggered ideas are:

- Talk about all the other ways we engender trust from our customers.
- Be at the forefront of privacy and security and start an open discussion around the subject.
- Be the thought leaders on relevant topics to show how openly we put privacy and security at the core of our business.

3 What are some specific measures the different world applies? How can you use these principles for your issue?

'The presenter's face is shown on billboards and social media so the listeners can put a face to a voice. They often perform public functions like attending goodwill events. Shows generally go out live so it's hard to cover up when something goes wrong. They deliberately provoke people to be involved by bringing in many viewpoints – even extreme ones.'

Triggered ideas are:

- Make security a personal issue for one of the executive team and publicise the responsible person's name.
- Make data security a differentiated feature of our service over that of our competitors.
- Make security a subject that our people feel they want to be close to – as if they would want to embrace it passionately.

4 If a professional from this industry were to take control of your area, what changes would they make to address your issue from their expertise perspective?

'Put the key people in the business in the public spotlight. Allow people to call in to speak to them. Make them accessible to the public through numerous channels.'

Triggered ideas are:

- Have this person involved in open communications about what measures the company is taking to safeguard data without risking security issues.
- Start a discussion inside the business about how data could be protected by inviting professionals from different facets of security to give advice.
- Consider getting a professional hacker on-board to help protect our systems from other hackers.

5 What is something unusual or unique to this different world in regard to how they handle their version of your issue? How can this be applied to your benefit?

'They put everything out on the airwaves live, so it's very hard to have privacy. Callers can use false names and nobody ever knows. Sometimes there is a few seconds delay to allow for censoring any bad language.'

Triggered ideas are:

- Have live updates of the latest viruses/hoaxes that are being used to steal identities and personal information, and offer precautions that can be taken.

- Can all password entries have a delay of a few seconds to ensure that automated multiple password attempts can't occur in just milliseconds – but would take years?

- Introduce time delays on password attempts after a number of incorrect attempts – much like on an iPhone.

Completing this tool

Once you've completed this tool, mark all the ideas you've generated with the notation 'B' in the top-right corner of the Genius Spaces where you've been writing your ideas – as shown below. This reminds you that these ideas relate to CHALLENGING area 'B'.

Tips on using this tool

You don't have to be an expert in any of the different worlds – what you know as a customer will be sufficient for developing interesting insights. This tool is similar to the Abstract. Move. Steal! tool where you look for activities already being done and just adapt them to your needs. Sometimes, your first impressions of how another world would handle your industry may seem peculiar – but capture them and try to use them as these could be of real value to you.

Tool 8: Three-Word Sentence

This is a technique that forces you to re-state the core essence of the issue and then to modify this expression in different ways.

Having to distil your CHALLENGING area into just three words helps you to drive to the core of the issue, which is then re-formed and re-phrased repeatedly to help you gain different viewpoints on how your issue could be interpreted differently.

How the tool works

Your CHALLENGING area needs to be re-constructed into a three-word sentence. Once this is done, the three words are entered into a table and five alternative words are listed for each of the stated words to complete the table. Then random combinations of words are used to stimulate and trigger new perspectives on the CHALLENGING area.

An example of the tool in use

Let's assume that you've taken the CHALLENGING area 'C' and re-formatted your Killer Question to be:

How can we get more time in a day to do all the things we need to do while at work?

This could be re-written as the three-word sentence: MAKE MORE TIME. These three words are then entered in the top three boxes in the tool frame on the template. You then need to list five alternate words in the columns below for each of the top three words. The words shouldn't have the identical meaning but should be similar to, or aligned to, the original word.

For example, words that could be added below MAKE might be build, acquire, buy, generate and manufacture. It's always good to include some unusual ones too, which in this case could be swap, spawn, assemble or invent. The table below uses a mix of these and also shows the other two columns completed.

Tool 8: Three-Word Sentence

The amended Killer Question is...

How can we get more time in a day to do all the things we need to do while at work?

1	MAKE	MORE	TIME
2	Acquire	Extra	Occasions
3	Buy	Spare	Spaces
4	Manufacture	Higher	Pace
5	Swap	Larger	Points
6	Invent	Many	Lives

You'll notice that MAKE is a verb and so all the words in this first column are verbs. Similarly, MORE is an adjective and TIME is a noun, so the words in the second and third columns should be adjectives and nouns respectively. This helps to ensure that no matter what combination of words are generated, they will always form a proper short sentence in a similar format to the original.

A dice is useful for creating random sentences. Imagine it is rolled three times and the numbers six, two and four come up.

Tool 8: Three-Word Sentence

The amended Killer Question is...

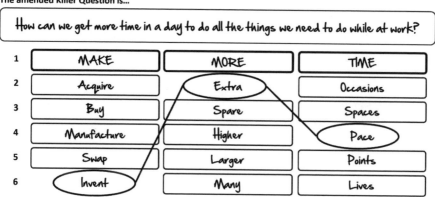

How can we get more time in a day to do all the things we need to do while at work?

1	MAKE	MORE	TIME
2	Acquire	Extra	Occasions
3	Buy	Spare	Spaces
4	Manufacture	Higher	Pace
5	Swap	Larger	Points
6	Invent	Many	Lives

This would create the sentence 'Invent Extra Pace'. This might suggest ideas around shortening meetings by having stand-up meetings or even meetings while you walk. What if the maximum meeting time was set at 30 minutes and no more?

Other dice rolls may produce the sentence 'Make Larger Occasions', which might suggest you being in a fixed location for an hour and six people can each get a ten-minute meeting slot with you. Or what if several managers did this in one room so you can get someone's immediate opinion or input on something without having to set up a subsequent meeting?

Alternatively, the dice may produce 'Swap Higher Points', which may trigger thinking on the quality of presentations. Imagine if internal presentations didn't need to be carefully formatted with images but could be just the cold hard facts without the visual design and formatting which takes up too much wasted time.

And finally the sentence 'Buy Spare Time' could trigger thinking around some kind of reward for people who finished meetings early, and to put practices in place in the business to prevent inefficient meetings.

Completing this tool

A reminder that once you've completed this tool, mark all the ideas you've generated with the notation 'C' in the Genius Spaces where you've been writing your ideas.

Tips on using this tool

This can be a tricky tool to use at first sight because the sentences don't make sense. However, if you feel that you want to roll the dice again to get a better sentence – don't! You need to make the mental effort to form the hard connections to stimulate fresh thinking – and not just taking the easy option of rolling the dice again. Even if the selection is peculiar, try to get at least two ideas from it before rolling another combination.

Tool 9: Your Alter Ego

This involves applying some deeply held personal perspectives from your alter ego – also known as your 'second self', and a personality which is distinct and different from your normal personality.

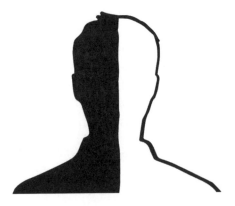

Your usual work personality is how you appear to others in the work environment; however, you have a life outside of work – and also a previous work life prior to your current role. These different lives represent your alter ego – the personality that nobody in your current work environment would normally ever see. It's these other personal lives that you can use to apply your thinking differently to any given work issue.

Part of your ability to be creative is the fact that you are different from other people in your company. Your job history prior to your current role is different to anybody else's and so your range of experiences is different too. Similarly when you consider your personal situation, social activities and interests – you are a very different person to everybody else – and this is where you can dig deeper for sources of personal creative differentiation.

How the tool works

From the project set-up, take the CHALLENGING area 'D' and rewrite your Killer Question to match it. Then think of some aspects of your life that are quite different from those your colleagues might consider if they were involved in this thinking project. You don't have to reveal what the differences are – that's personal to you. But highlight some key differentiators and think how using these as the basis for fresh perspectives can help you see things in ways that nobody else can.

The alter ego considerations you can use are:

1 Previous roles you have had before you joined your current company or even moved into the industry you currently work in.
2 The hobbies, pastimes or social activities you enjoy.
3 Review how people you admire and respect in your work and social lives would approach this issue.
4 What's an analogy in your non-work life where you've previously overcome an issue with great success?

Here's the tool as it appears in the template:

Tool 9: Your Alter Ego

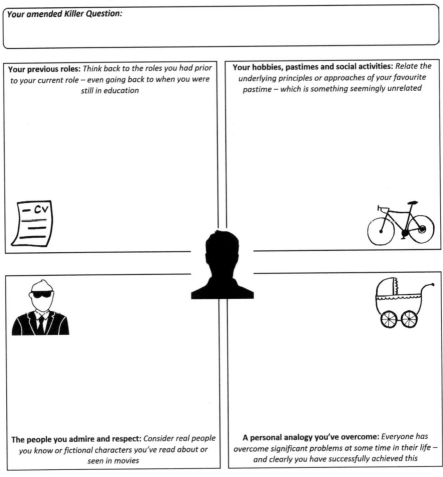

Your amended Killer Question:

Your previous roles: *Think back to the roles you had prior to your current role – even going back to when you were still in education*

Your hobbies, pastimes and social activities: *Relate the underlying principles or approaches of your favourite pastime – which is something seemingly unrelated*

The people you admire and respect: *Consider real people you know or fictional characters you've read about or seen in movies*

A personal analogy you've overcome: *Everyone has overcome significant problems at some time in their life – and clearly you have successfully achieved this*

For each of the alter ego quadrants, note down some relevant items for that theme and consider how your issue could be addressed using this alter ego insight as a thinking trigger.

An example of the tool in use

Rather than relate this exercise to a specific issue, let's consider how this technique can be applied generically to any given situation.

1 **Your previous roles:** Think back to the roles you had prior to your current role – even going back to when you were still in education.

   - When did a similar analogous situation exist – and what did you do to overcome it?
   - What were the standard approaches used in another industry/ business that you are familiar with for this type of issue?
   - How were their attitudes and focus different to what you are considering today?

2 **Your hobbies, pastimes and social activities:** Relate the underlying principles or approaches of your favourite pastime – which is something seemingly unrelated – and apply them to addressing your issue.

   - For an avid soccer fan it could be how a team creates set-piece plays for different situations or the role of each player in a team and how this can be relevant to the current situation.
   - For a nature lover it may be how specific animals, plants or insects interact together to form a symbiotic environment in the natural world.
   - If you are involved with your church, youth organisations or charity work, how could the principles of operation and interaction in these situations be relevant to the work issue you want to address?

3 **The people you admire and respect:** Consider real people you know or fictional characters you've read about or seen in movies.

   - What would their approach to this issue be?
   - How would they extract the key issues to be addressed and what type of action would they take to resolve them?
   - Even consider some 'extreme' characters who you wouldn't let anywhere near your business. What valuable insights can you gain from their character or potential approaches?

4 **A personal analogy you've overcome:** Everyone has overcome significant problems at some time in their life – and clearly you have successfully achieved this.

   - How have you approached personal difficulties in your life previously and how can those approaches and solution methods be of benefit now?

- You may have overcome a dread disease or physical disability at some time. How did your attitude and the various treatments and support systems interact with you – and how could this be analogous and useful to the thinking situation you now face?
- What family-related issues are similar to the one you are addressing now, and how do you handle them?

Completing this tool

When you've completed this tool, identify all your ideas with the notation 'D' in the Genius Spaces where you've been writing your ideas.

Tips on using this tool

You have had a life that is very different to anybody else's – unique in fact. And the way you have overcome issues in the past is probably attributable to the approach you took and the methods involved in remedying your situation. Your past – though it may seem quite irrelevant to the issue you are considering now – is of great value to you, and to you alone. So make the most of it.

Tool 10: Black and White Thinking

It may intuitively feel right that the 'middle ground' is where the optimum solutions exist, but sometimes the middle ground is just a wasteland of mediocrity. This tool helps you to deconstruct an issue into some core components and then to rebuild it into a more relevant and focused solution.

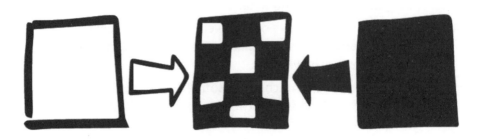

Imagine that your issue has two key aspects, one of which is black, at one end of a spectrum, while the second is white at the other end of the spectrum. A perfect solution that combines both these aspects might be deemed to sit at the mid-point on the spectrum, and the mid-point between black and white is grey – the effect when you mix the colours black and white.

If some people desire the black aspects of your offer and others desire the white aspects, you may think that your mid-point grey solution satisfies both types of people. However, there's a problem, because grey doesn't satisfy the needs of those that want black, and neither does it satisfy the needs of those that want white. While grey may intuitively feel to be the best thing to offer – it isn't. Rather than mix the two colours to get grey, we need to create a chequerboard effect that has black aspects for those that want black and also white aspects for those that want white. The chequerboard is the better solution – not the grey that we may have originally believed.

How the tool works

Take the CHALLENGING area 'E' that's under consideration and deconstruct it into four key, idealised, component parts. These component parts can represent any broad answers to your modified Killer Question that you might regard as being a success. They are your ideal or desired outcomes – not specific ways to achieve these outcomes. The example below demonstrates this. There may be more than four component parts that you can identify, but simply list as many as you can and then select the four that you believe to be the most important, or which have the greatest potential for success in some way. List them and number them from one to four. This is not a ranking; it's just a way to identify them individually.

You then create a matrix which helps you to match each one of these in turn with the other three, and each time you do it's a chance to see what interesting connections and combinations arise. Here's how the generic matrix is structured:

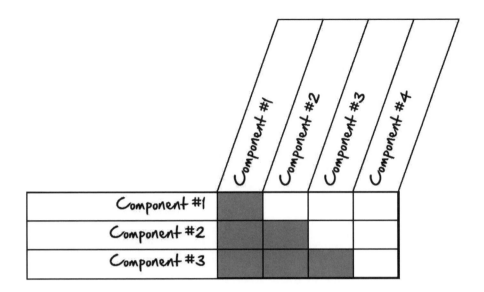

This is like the black and white chequerboard approach except using four colours and making different colour-combination chequerboards from different pairs of colours.

An example of the tool in use

Imagine that your re-written Killer Question based around your CHALLENGING area 'E' is:

How can we increase the level of diversity in our business at senior management levels?

Then list as many key component parts that represent ideal outcomes to this issue as you can. In this example the components may be:

- Attract new people
- Develop people from within
- Increase gender balance
- Introduce job sharing
- Be appealing to the minority groups we need
- Increase ethnic balance
- Implement affirmative action policies

- Create a support network
- Retain the best
- Convert consultants to permanent staff

Let's assume that in this particular example the four most relevant components (in no particular order) are:

1 Attract new people
2 Increase gender balance
3 Create a support network
4 Retain the best

These can be entered onto the matrix model that you'll find in the templates and a completed example is shown below:

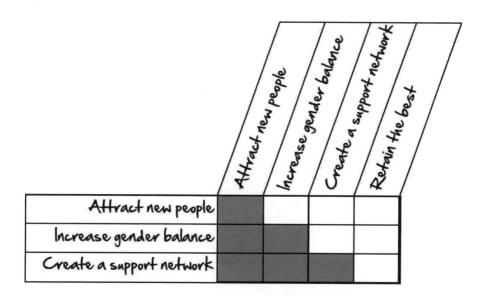

You will notice that some of the elements of the matrix are greyed-out. This is where the same components are being referenced together or where there is a duplication of interaction – and so these interactions can be omitted.

If you look at the first active intersection on the top row of the matrix, you can now consider what interesting ideas arise from 'Attract new people' and 'Increase gender balance'. Ways to recruit suitable women could be to appoint them as designates for specific senior roles, or to recruit mid-level women and immediately put them on a fast-track development programme. Alternatively, you could implement other female-friendly protocols in the business which might include incentivising the male employees to do the socialising to win the business while the women can work more friendly/flexible hours to develop or deliver on the relationship.

As another example of the six intersections on the matrix, take where 'Create a support network' intersects with 'Retain the best'. Here you could have each person mentored by a senior internal or external woman to aid them in their development. There could even be a share option scheme that is only for the select group of women within the support network, which encourages them all to work together for the good of the company but also for the betterment of their private group. Other examples may be some innovative approaches to flexible working arrangements allowing home working as and when needed. Similarly, accepting that women have greater personal care needs than men, have facilities on site for certain services that are more suited to women than men.

You'll notice that these ideas are focused around women – which is a continuation of the focus from the first example. But they could just as easily be made relevant to any group of employees you are trying to grow.

Completing this tool

Don't forget to mark all the ideas you've generated with the notation 'E' in the small boxes to indicate that these ideas relate to CHALLENGING area 'E'.

Tips on using this tool

Be wary of just focusing on the individual component parts alone, for while this is important, it's the intersections of the components that are important and which can drive out some new and interesting insights to deliver success.

An additional tip to using this toolset is to apply your subconscious to the issue. As another example from this tool, imagine that you wanted to consider what personal care facilities you could have in your corporate offices to appeal to female employees so they considered your company as one of the most female-friendly businesses in the city. Let this issue dwell in your subconscious to see what interesting ideas come to you at odd moments. Additionally, while you are commuting to or from work, or while doing other activities around town, keep this question bubbling in your subconscious and note down any ideas that occur to you based on what you see, hear and experience.

The subconscious is a very powerful tool and an excellent supplementary thinking technique when used well. All you have to do is have a question that you need answering, and to let it dwell. Your subconscious can deliver surprising results for you.

Assessment and building stage

You'll see how the five tools have been applied to the five CHALLENGING areas that you identified at the start of this Divide and Conquer toolset. By leapfrogging the EXHAUSTED areas you've avoided wasting time covering the previously, well-trodden ground and have been able to spend your thinking time and effort in more useful areas.

As you completed each tool you were asked to mark each idea developed for that tool with the appropriate letter 'A' to 'E'. You now know which ideas relate to which tool – and so to which CHALLENGING area.

You will now review your outputs for each of the tools in turn and select the three ideas that you believe offer greatest potential for answering the Killer Question for that tool. On the template you can write your CHALLENGING area 'A' in the upper space and then write your top three ideas marked 'A' in the three boxes just below. Write the idea you are most excited about in the first space, the next most exciting idea in the next space and third most exciting idea in the final space. Then look at how you might integrate or combine these, or add something else to make one or more boosted ideas that may be even more compelling that the original ideas you had. A completed example is shown below.

Divide and Conquer: SUMMARY

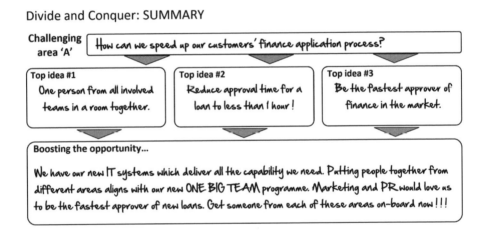

Challenging area 'A'

How can we speed up our customers' finance application process?

Top idea #1

One person from all involved teams in a room together.

Top idea #2

Reduce approval time for a loan to less than 1 hour!

Top idea #3

Be the fastest approver of finance in the market.

Boosting the opportunity...

We have our new IT systems which deliver all the capability we need. Putting people together from different areas aligns with our new ONE BIG TEAM programme. Marketing and PR would love us to be the fastest approver of new loans. Get someone from each of these areas on-board now!!!

Avoid simply merging the three ideas into one solution as this frequently tends to lose some of the sparkle that the individual ideas may have had. Instead, aim to add more value by creating additional ideas that may be even better than the three you initially developed.

Then perform a similar exercise for the other four CHALLENGING areas in the remaining summary spaces on the template. Once you've completed this exercise you will have some exciting opportunities that address each of the five CHALLENGING areas of your Killer Question. These may be interesting opportunities on their own – or you may want to undertake an exercise to integrate and boost these five areas into one over-arching solution. You can decide what's the best course of action to take based on your immediate needs and situation.

Remember to formulate your outputs as winning ideas that attract other people towards them. Re-read the section on shaping your winning ideas if necessary.

Boundary Riding (thinking tools 11–15)

The Boundary Riding toolset helps you to identify ways to organically grow your business in the short to medium timeframes. To achieve this, the toolset assumes that you will not be looking for radically new areas of business as these will likely extend beyond the current capabilities of your people and resources and will take too long to develop. Instead, it focuses on identifying opportunities that are adjacent to what you do now.

The Boundary Riding template can be downloaded free of charge from: **www.TheIdeaGenerator.info**

Setting up your project

Boundary Riding applies one Killer Question to different elements of a single area of your business. This Killer Question is:

How might we grow [this part of our business] to achieve a significant increase in revenues over the next two to six months?

The 'part of the business' referred to in this Killer Question should generally relate to an area that you – or you and your team – have responsibility for. Unless you've been specifically requested by your senior management to explore for opportunities for a larger part of the business, applying your thinking efforts to the areas on which you are personally assessed represents your best chance for practical success.

The reference to 'increase in revenues' assumes that any growth achieved maintains the required business profit levels and isn't selling at any cost, which would increase revenues but diminish profit margins and hence overall profitability. The outputs will be a range of ideas, some of which will be quick wins that can be implemented immediately, while others will be for development over the short to medium term – which is assumed to be a two- to six-month time horizon – although this may vary for some industries. You will undoubtedly get some longer-term ideas that can form part of your future planning process too, but these aren't specifically targeted as outcomes for the Boundary Riding toolset. If you need to explore for longer term, more strategic opportunities then use either the Islands of Opportunity or the Divide and Conquer toolsets.

The tools focus on the boundaries of your current domain of business to see what opportunities exist just beyond them. It's likely there won't be just one opportunity identified, but that there will be several for you to consider. While some may be applicable to all products or services, it's more probable that specific opportunities will arise for individual aspects of your propositions.

All the Boundary Riding tools start by stating a specific focus for each tool. While the entire toolset is directed at a specific area of the business as defined by the Killer Question, there will undoubtedly be several different elements within that area that can be considered individually. These could be different products, product sets, services, proposition packages, customer types, service channels, and more.

The five tools within this toolset each enable you to select a different element at the start to help you creatively develop that element. This is referred to as the growth focus and there is a space at the start of each tool for you to write this in. This simple act of writing out your growth focus also helps to embed it within your subconscious.

Tool 11: Cracks in the Pavement

Sometimes you can be too close to an issue to notice some interesting aspects of it. This tool helps you to look inside the business at the existing activities to creatively identify some minor changes that can deliver significant additional benefits.

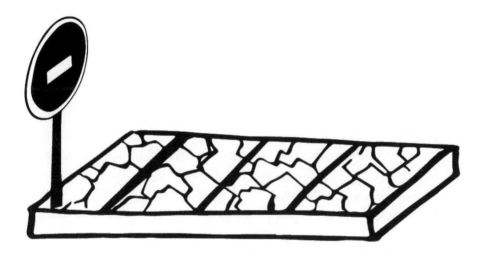

Imagine a pavement representing your business. Each paving stone signifying a product you sell or an operational part of your business that generates revenue. All too often your people might stand on the pavement and stare out to the distant horizons looking to identify some new revenue streams. However, there's often value right beneath your feet – in the cracks between the paving stones which is going unnoticed. For it's in these cracks that gold dust gathers, and we often miss this because we are too focused on the far horizon – which naturally seems more interesting and exciting than staring at your feet.

How the tool works

Cracks in the Pavement helps you identify practical changes you can make to an existing product or service by examining it closely to see what marginal modifications might deliver big revenue opportunities. This is achieved using a MARISA approach, where MARISA is an acronym which stands for *Magnify, Add, Rationalise, Integrate, Speed-up* and *Adapt*. Each of these terms has a series of considerations to apply to re-evaluate the product or service. The full list of considerations within the tool is as follows:

- **Magnify:** How can a part of this be made bigger, longer, broader, more encompassing, more expensive, better, amplified, increased, heightened or extended?

- **Add:** Where can something be attached, included, enhanced, bolted-on, augmented, supplemented, enlarged or complemented?

- **Rationalise:** What can be removed, destroyed, eliminated, simplified, streamlined, downsized, cut back, watered down or reduced?

- **Integrate:** When can things be merged, shared, joined up, linked together, mixed up, fused, combined, entangled or amalgamated?

- **Speed-up:** How can something be accelerated, made faster, have steps removed, boosted, assisted, arrive sooner, be closer or be shorter?

- **Adapt:** What can be made lighter, split up, reversed, upgraded, downgraded, moved sideways, de-scoped, adjusted or automated?

Select one specific element of your business (it could be a product or service) and enter it into the 'growth focus' space at the top of the Cracks in the Pavement page on the template. The focus for this tool is entirely on this one product or service, and there's room in the template to draw a sketch, diagram, process or outline of the product or service to help you to see it differently. It's not often you do this, but give it a try as it will get some previously unused neurons firing in your brain. Here's how the tool appears in the template:

Tool 11: Cracks in the Pavement

> *The growth focus*
> *for this tool is...*

Draw a sketch of it here in whatever form helps you to imagine it more clearly or in an interesting manner.

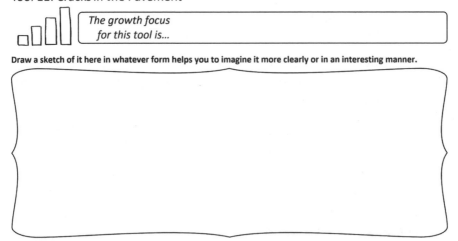

Now apply MARISA to it...

Magnify: How can a part of this be made bigger, longer, broader, more encompassing, more expensive, better, amplified, increased, heightened or extended?

Add: Where can something be attached, included, enhanced, bolted-on, augmented, supplemented, enlarged or complemented?

Rationalise: What can be removed, destroyed, eliminated, simplified, streamlined, downsized, cut back, watered down or reduced?

Integrate: When can things be merged, shared, joined up, linked together, mixed up, fused, combined, entangled or amalgamated?

Speed-up: How can something be accelerated, made faster, have steps removed, boosted, assisted, arrive sooner, be closer or be shorter?

Adapt: What can be made lighter, split up, reversed, upgraded, downgraded, moved sideways, de-scoped, adjusted or automated?

Now interrogate it with each of the MARISA considerations and capture any interesting ideas that can be applied to your growth focus in your Genius Spaces.

An example of the tool in use

If one of the services that you offer is . . .

Providing building and facilities management for corporate office blocks . . . then some things to consider using the components of the MARISA tool could be:

Magnify: How can a part of this be made bigger, longer, broader, more encompassing, more expensive, better, amplified, increased, heightened or extended?

- Extend into maintenance of the grounds around the building.
- Offer deep-cleaning, sanitisation services in the winter months to clean telephones, keyboards, door-handles etc. to reduce the risk of cold and flu germs being spread during this time.
- Offer a courier service for inter-office deliveries and/or a bus service between the various buildings.

Add: Where can something be attached, included, enhanced, bolted-on, augmented, supplemented, enlarged or complemented?

- Include servicing, valeting and detailing of company vehicles.
- Be the source of qualified advice on minimising the spread of illnesses in office buildings and what staff can do to minimise the risk to themselves and others.
- Offer a confidential document shredding service.

Rationalise: What can be removed, destroyed, eliminated, simplified, streamlined, downsized, cut back, watered down or reduced?

- Reduce the security risk to clients by replacing numerous smaller suppliers of services around the building, e.g. plant care.
- Manage the routine refreshing of the reception area with fresh flowers, magazines, marketing collateral etc.
- Take over the in-building refilling of the vending machines, or even become a supplier of the vending machines and their services.

Integrate: When can things be merged, shared, joined up, linked together, mixed up, fused, combined, entangled or amalgamated?

- Manage the staff cafes in buildings (people and operation).
- Source proprietary branded food products when we manage sufficient cafes to warrant this.
- Engage staff in healthy eating programmes by providing appropriate meals and diet-support mechanisms.

Speed-up: How can something be accelerated, made faster, have steps removed, boosted, assisted, arrive sooner, be closer or be shorter?

- Offer a concierge service to take visitors to their meeting point to save time for staff having to do this.
- Offer a check-in app for visitors to allow them to provide all the information regarding their meeting before they arrive.
- Be the experts in what to do in the event of an emergency or incident in the building to ensure the safety and protection of people and assets.

Adapt: What can be made lighter, split up, reversed, upgraded, downgraded, moved sideways, de-scoped, adjusted or automated?

- Develop the skills and expertise to manage all functions that are non-core to the delivery of the company's business.
- Include exterior maintenance of the buildings.
- Offer energy efficient audits and cost-saving exercises for the buildings being managed.

Tips on using this tool

You can apply this approach to any customer proposition that you offer. However, the tool works best when you focus on one specific aspect of your business and interrogate it deeply and thoroughly. Once you have completed it for one product, service, or other element you can then apply it a second time to another one if you so desire.

Tool 12: Four Customer Lenses

Pushing the boundaries of your engagement with a specific type of customer in new ways and at deeper levels by focusing on it from the customer's perspective.

You tend not to interfere with things that aren't broken – but sometimes, things that appear to be working reasonably well can benefit from an extra boost. This tool poses four powerful questions that help to deepen your relationship with a target group of customers.

How the tool works

Identify the product, service or other element that you will focus on for this tool and enter it into the 'growth focus' space on the template. You will be using a persona as part of this tool to help you consider this element from the customer's perspective and not from the usual business perspective.

A persona is a mini-biography of a fictional individual who represents a specific type of customer (called a customer segment) or even a type of person who isn't a current customer. It helps you to understand them so you can target your marketing and interaction activities accordingly – so they appeal to them in the most effective manner.

Some companies have developed formal personas for their different customer segments – but if your company doesn't have any, then that's not a problem. You can create a persona very quickly using the persona framework which guides you through the development of one. This helps you to be more focused on a specific type of customer rather than trying to think around some generic customer – who in all likelihood doesn't exist.

There are two Persona Frameworks in the template which are very similar in nature. The first is a consumer persona for when your customer is a member of the public – or an end-consumer. The second is for a business-to-business (B2B) relationship where the customer is an individual who is dealing with you on behalf of the company they work for. The differences between the two types of persona are clearly indicated on the frameworks. The B2B version as it appears in the template is shown here as this is the one used in the upcoming example:

Tool 12: Persona Framework – *business customer*

| Customer: ☐ | Non-customer: ☐ | | Male: ☐ | Female: ☐ | | Age: [   ] |

Their name: [   ]   **Their role:** [   ]

An outline of the company they work for:

A brief work biography of the person:

How they interact with your company:

What they like and dislike about dealing with your industry:

When setting up a business persona, decide whether the individual will be a current customer or a non-customer, and then choose their gender and the age this type of person may typically be. Give them a name (first name and surname) and also state the job role that they have at their company. This should represent the type of person who normally makes the purchase decision to use your product or service.

Next, detail the company they work for and expand on the type of work they do and how this relates to the products or services you provide. Add some information regarding your persona's work background at their company, such as how long they've been there, how long they've worked in the industry, and what other roles (if any) they perform in the company. Include detail on how your persona actually interacts with your business. Do they use the products themselves or buy them for others to use, and how do they order and re-order from you? How is delivery or collection made and who is involved in authorising the purchase and accepting the delivery?

Finally, add some background on how your persona, and the type of company they work for, regard your business and the industry you are in. Do they consider your business and industry from a positive or negative perspective? Are the interactions remote and automated or are they more personal in nature – and how do they feel about the type of people they have to deal with in your business or industry?

Once you have your persona identified, you then consider three key interactions that you have with this type of customer, namely the way your persona becomes aware of your product or service; how they buy or order it; and the way they engage with you after they've purchased it.

Before a customer can ever consider buying something from you, they have to be aware of several things. They need to know that your company exists in the first instance; to understand what you sell or do; and that your company and your products and services are appropriate to their needs. Only then might they consider a purchase. At this point they need to decide how they wish to buy or order your product or service and what channels they will use to do this. Once the purchase is complete there are the ways in which they engage with you in the short and longer terms with regard to their purchase. What happens in the short term if they have an issue with their purchase – and how do you interact with them on an ongoing basis for consumables, spares, servicing and renewal?

To help understand these interactions in more detail, you now apply Four Customer Lenses to study, interrogate and boost each one of them to see how they can be optimised for the benefit of your persona in some way.

The four customer lenses used are:

1   What's the one thing that when stopped will make this better?
2   What's a small change that will ripple over several areas?
3   What will make this twice as effective?
4   What's a change that will deliver a quantum-leap benefit?

This is how this tool appears in the template. Note that only the awareness interaction is shown here:

Tool 12: Four Customer Lenses

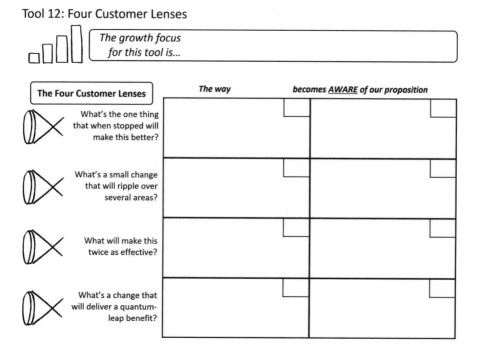

You can add the ideas that are triggered directly into the Genius Spaces provided to the right of the four lenses.

An example of the tool in use

Imagine that your company provides IT security services for small to medium-sized businesses, and your Killer Question is:

How do we rapidly grow the uptake of the new range of 'hacker defence' services that we've developed?

If your business uses formal customer personas, then select and use one of these as the customer you will apply the tool to. If you don't have formal personas, then you must create one. Your persona can include someone from one of your main customer segments or it can represent a customer segment where you aren't well represented and which offers significant potential for growth.

In this example persona, it's assumed that the focus is on a current customer segment.

Persona overview

Jenny Watson is 42 years old, female, a current customer of ours, and she's an information technology (IT) manager.

Outline of her company

Jenny works at the County Housing Trust which manages and operates a number of social housing projects and developments around the county. Her organisation provides a range of services to various sub-organisations that run and maintain 3200 housing units.

Brief work biography

Jenny is the IT manager for the housing trust. She works at the head office where they employ around 90 people. She's a full-time employee there and has been with her current organisation for over six years. She makes all the recommendations on what to do regarding their IT activities but she has to get any non-budgeted expenditure approved by the head of finance.

How they interact with us

Jenny has another role as project manager in the organisation and so is only involved in the IT side part-time. She has a good knowledge of the day-to-day IT issues that the organisation's employees have and is competent at resolving them. However, she's not very confident at the bigger IT issues they might face and frequently asks us for advice. She's been using our data back-up service for the last four years. One of our technicians will usually go to help her set up any new services she buys from us.

What they like and dislike about dealing with us

Jenny trusts us because our back-up service is robust and the few times they've needed to recover old data, we've enabled them to do this quickly and effectively. She sometimes doesn't understand that when she has a problem we can't always respond to her immediately – but we always respond within 24 hours.

A quick way of creating a persona is to use the information you know about one of your actual customers as a proxy representation of a particular customer segment. If you are targeting people who don't currently use your products or services, then imagine the relationship they have with their current supplier – and why they don't use your company as their supplier.

This Four Customer Lenses exercise needs to get personal – so copy your persona's name into the blank spaces for each interaction in the tool, as this will help to keep you focused on the persona. An example of this is shown below where Jenny's name has been added.

Tool 12: Four Customer Lenses

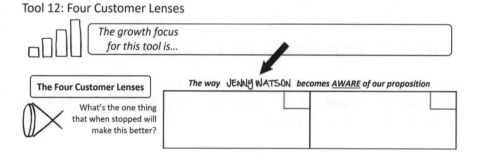

The first customer lens used on the template for the interaction 'The way Jenny becomes aware of our proposition' is 'What's the one thing that when stopped will make this better?' In this example, some ideas that you might have that will address this interaction are:

- Stop calling our product a 'Ransomware Defence Protocol' in our adverts and conversations. This sounds too technical, complex and expensive. Make it sound like something that won't scare Jenny away.

- Stop talking generically about the 'risk' and 'cost' of a hacker gaining access to their systems and instead create a case study that gives some specific values in terms of financial cost, reputation cost, recovery cost, lost data cost etc. for various sizes of small and medium-sized businesses.

- Stop talking about hackers nebulously and quote the numbers of fraudulent access attempts as publically stated by some of the world's leading security software developers.

- Stop using a broad geographical approach and refer to an actual case of a *local* business that was held to ransom by a hacker who remotely installed a virus on their computer system.

Tips on using this tool

Complete the Four Customer Lenses for one interaction before continuing on to the second and third interactions. These interactions are a sequential representation of your persona's progressive engagement with your business, so do them in order. Try to put yourself into the shoes – and full character – of your persona as you complete this tool.

Tool 13: The Do-It-Yourself Business

If your company formed a number of new, stand-alone business units, each focused around delivering one specific product or service, how might things be done differently?

My Business (Ltd)

The aim is to identify what approaches you would take if the scenario around this particular product or service was very different. Consider that you are one of five people nominated as the potential managing director for one of these business units. You are in competition for the role and only one of you can be successful. You will be judged on the creative ideas you come up with for growing this particular product or service as a standalone business. So you have to pro-actively and creatively out-think the other four candidates. What would you propose?

This tool puts you at the front and centre of shaping a business opportunity based on your personal experiences of what approaches you'd take, and what you know works well. It encourages you to rethink through an existing product or service but from the perspective of being totally unconstrained by conventional approaches, unhindered by the existing beliefs and considerations, and having a clean-sheet opportunity to what you could do to make this product or service a massive success.

You can apply this tool to one of your main product or service propositions that you currently offer to customers, or you could consider one of your smaller, focused propositions and use this as your base for growth for a new business. The choice is yours.

How the tool works

If you were launching a new business there are many things that you'd need to contemplate – but here you will focus solely on those related to the specific product or service you have selected. First, you need to enter the product or service of your choice into the growth focus space at the beginning of the tool.

You will now interrogate this product or service with a series of considerations that will identify potential levers for change that may offer massive opportunities for you. These considerations for your product or service are:

- **Fundamental Purpose:** Reflect on the fundamental purpose of the product or service. What's a change in this that would offer more value to customers? How might this be different for some new customers that you haven't yet attracted?

- **Prior Activity:** What things do the users of your service do immediately before they use this product or service? How can you incorporate or extend this into your proposition? What's an innovative way to add additional value here for both you and the customer?

- **Post Activity:** Similarly, what things do the users of your service do immediately after they use this product or service? How can you include this activity into your proposition somehow to add greater value here for both you and the customer?

- **Analogous Situation:** What's an analogous situation from a completely different industry – and what do they do differently to you? How could you apply this principle to your situation to generate additional value for the key stakeholders involved?

- **Stripped Back:** If you were to strip away all the other current aspects of your business that are wrapped up with this product or service to make it a truly stand-alone entity, how might this be presented as a powerful proposition to potential customers? How would this stripped back and simplified product or service appeal to customers compared to the competitor's propositions that are available in the market?

- **Joined Offer:** Consider the stripped-back product above, what one thing when added or combined with it will make an amazing new proposition? Alternatively, if you were to combine this with another product or service offered by someone else either inside or outside of your current company, how could this become a brilliant new offer in the market?

The structure of this tool in the template is shown below:

Tool 13: The Do-It-Yourself Business

The growth focus for this tool is...

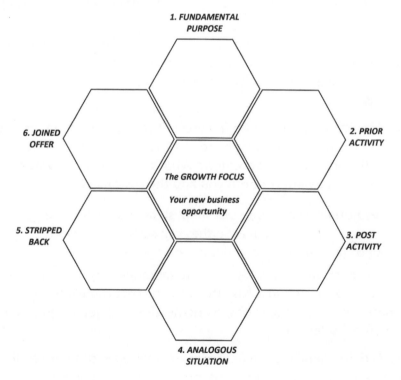

1. FUNDAMENTAL PURPOSE

6. JOINED OFFER

2. PRIOR ACTIVITY

The GROWTH FOCUS

Your new business opportunity

5. STRIPPED BACK

3. POST ACTIVITY

4. ANALOGOUS SITUATION

This 'competitive' new business venture approach to thinking of this issue will help you to identify some differentiated opportunities and approaches that you could apply now as part of your normal course of business.

An example of the tool in use

If you were a supplier of consumer electrical goods and wanted to create a separate business for the home entertainment range of products you sell, then this is how some of the considerations may be answered.

Fundamental Purpose: Reflect on the fundamental purpose of the item. What's a change in this that would offer more value to customers? How might this be different for some new customers that you haven't yet attracted?

- It's about the entertainment they will experience in their own homes – so we should go to their homes to explain the packages we offer.
- Do a survey of the number of hours of enjoyment they get from home entertainment and spread the cost of any new spending on our products over a year or more on a cost-per-day-per-person basis.

Prior Activity: What things do the users of your service do immediately before they use this product or service? How can you incorporate or extend this into your proposition? What's an innovative way to add additional value here for both you and the customer?

- They normally come into our shop, so take top-of-the-range products into their homes so they can see how they look and sound. Take an order and deposit on the spot.
- They do research on what content packages they may want to watch, so we should advise them on the best cable/Internet TV package for their type of viewing needs – and get a commission on these sales.

Post Activity: Similarly, what things do the users of your service do immediately after they use this product or service? How can you include this activity into your proposition somehow to add greater value here for both you and the customer?

- Advise them of new services they may not be aware of across all aspects of home entertainment – not just our TVs.
- Follow up after a period of one or three months and offer them sales options to 'partner' entertainment services so they get even greater enjoyment from their purchases.

Analogous Situation: What's an analogous situation from a completely different industry – and what do they do differently to you? How could you apply this principle to your situation to generate additional value for the key stakeholders involved?

- Insurance companies have online calculators to work out the premium cost – so do a similar thing where it shows how low the cost-per-person-per-day is for a great TV experience.
- Kitchen installers leave everything complete and ready to use – so we can do the same with our installations – even download some of their favourite shows or series for them.

Stripped Back: If you were to strip away all the other current aspects of your business that are wrapped up with this product or service to make it a truly stand-alone entity, how might this be presented as a powerful proposition to potential customers? How would this stripped-back and simplified product or service appeal to customers compared to the competitor's propositions that are available in the market?

- Sell and install 'pure entertainment' to customers as that's what they really want – and our equipment can help them to get this.
- Offer to remove and dispose of their old equipment to keep their home clear of old technology.

Joined Offer: Consider the stripped-back product above, what one thing when added or combined with it will make an amazing new proposition? Alternatively, if you were to combine this with another product or service offered by someone else, either inside or outside of your business, how could this be a brilliant new market offer?

- While installing the equipment, leave behind some brochures regarding other non-entertainment products we sell that are cutting edge in purpose or design. We can try to profile our customers based on what they initially bought from us.

- Have a link to a partner supplier who builds customised TV cabinets to make their products more functional with regard to appearance and storage of DVDs, CDs, devices etc.

Tips on using this tool

If your company were to create separate business units for the various core offers, it would be a radical move to make, so your thinking approach to how you would creatively address this change also needs to be quite radical in nature – but with a pragmatic twist. Your existing structure and systems around these products will naturally impede your thinking, so be bold in your approaches to break through the existing barriers of what's actually happening and is usually done.

Tool 14: The Quirky Equation

This is a structured approach which brings four elements of a business engagement together in an unusual equation to form a new and enhanced over-arching proposition for your customers.

$$I = \frac{B}{(t + D)^E}$$

Fresh opportunities for four components of a customer proposition are brought together in different combinations to help define a fifth component which is the desirable end result for your business, namely *Excellence in results*.

How the tool works

Begin by entering the growth focus for this tool into the space on the template. Next you need to list all the interesting and advantageous assets that you possess as a business. These may include skills or competencies that you have that are above average and which could be leveraged for greater benefit, or they are those things which you own or have rights to use, or access to, that your competitors don't. These items could relate to your location; your brand; your reputation; your service or product rating; your size; some intellectual property that you own; a partnership or relationship that you have with another party; or any number of other items that you believe offer you a distinct advantage over your competitors.

As an example, if you owned a new car dealership within a region for a luxury car brand, then some of your advantageous assets might be:

- The fact you have new models regularly released
- You offer environmentally friendly, hybrid fuel models
- You can loan trial cars to potential buyers
- Your service centres have won awards
- You also sell recent, pre-owned vehicles
- You have a prestigious brand and a long, heritage reputation
- You have great showroom locations serving a large metropolitan area
- You have a close relationship with an advanced driving school

List anything that you consider as an advantageous asset for your business – even if it initially seems remote to the growth focus for this tool.

The Quirky Equation itself is **A + B + C + D = E** where:

- **A = Amazing difference:** What will make this amazingly different to whatever the current situation is?
- **B = Business value:** What things will help this to deliver exceptional 'business value' to your organisation?
- **C = Customer desire:** What will make this desirable to customers?
- **D = Dead certainty:** What will help to make this an absolute certainty of success when it is executed?
- **E = Excellence in results:** What will a stunning result look like and how could it be delivered in a sensational manner?

For each of the first four parts of the equation, list three new and innovative ways to make that part of the equation a reality. Try to incorporate your advantageous assets in some way, as using these will (by default) create opportunities that your competition will find hard to copy.

Once all parts of the equation are complete, select combinations at random to see what thoughts and ideas they trigger to produce the answers to the fifth part of the equation. Here's how it looks in the template:

Tool 14: The Quirky Equation

> The growth focus
> for this tool is...

Our advantageous assets

-
-
-
-
-
-
-

-
-
-
-
-
-
-

Amazing difference + **B**usiness value + **C**ustomer desire + **D**ead certainty = **E**xcellence in results

What elements of a solution could produce an *Amazing difference*?

1.
2.
3.

+

What elements of a solution could produce significant *Business value*?

4.
5.
6.

+

What elements of a solution could produce massive *Customer desire*?

7.
8.
9.

+

What elements of a solution could make this a *Dead certainty* for success?

10.
11.
12.

=

How do we combine these elements to produce and deliver *Excellence in results*?

An example of the tool in use

Imagine that the specific growth activity that you want to focus on is increasing the revenues from your heavy goods vehicle hire service.

The advantageous assets you have are:

- You work with some of the largest transport companies in the country
- You have relationships with some clients that have lasted many years
- You have five depots around the country
- Your depots work on a 24/7 and 365 days a year basis
- You have strong relationships with some heavy vehicle towing companies

You can now consider the various parts of the equation individually.

What elements of a solution could produce an *Amazing difference*?

1 Provide a fully serviced pay-per-mile vehicle hire including driver.

2 Add branded decals to stick on the cab doors so the client's brand appears on the vehicle.

3 Solve the customer's logistical issue by doing the entire delivery/transportation service for them.

What elements of a solution could produce significant *Business value*?

4 Include the hire of different types of trailer.

5 Offer to repaint and rebrand vehicles if the customer commits to a long-term hire relationship.

6 Form a relationship with the heavy vehicle recovery companies where they advise us of a broken-down vehicle and we can get a replacement truck to haul the trailer of the broken-down vehicle within a prescribed timeframe. This could form an insurance service for haulage operators especially where the cargo is chilled or needs a rapid delivery.

What elements of a solution could produce massive *Customer desire*?

7　Offer to outsource all their vehicle maintenance for them and provide the trucks (and possibly drivers too) on a wet-lease basis.

8　Offer guarantees in the form of service-level agreements for emergency hire that are the best in the hire business.

9　Have a specific person allocated to major accounts who they can contact in an emergency on a 24/7 basis.

What elements of a solution could make this a *Dead certainty* for success?

10　Demonstrate how it helps them to help their customers in an emergency.

11　Help clients to reduce the risk of a lost cargo (or even a lost contract) due to a major delay in the delivery time to their end-customers.

12　Offer the best haulage emergency delivery service in the country.

Some examples of developed *Excellence in results* could be:

- Combining #1 and #8 gives a simple payment structure that is based on the notice period given for the hire of a truck. An emergency request is charged at the highest rates while bookings made a week in advance are at the base costing. All rates are pre-agreed so the clients can work out exactly how much it will cost them.

- Combining #2, #3 and #5 gives the opportunity to help the client to be seen as a much bigger operation in that the trucks carry their branding – while we do all their logistical activity for them.

- Combining #6 and #11 gives the opportunity to be the 'delivery insurance' provider for the client that they can then pass on to *their* customers to help deliver a 'peace of mind promise' for their end-customers.

- Combining #7 and #10 gives the opportunity to relieve the clients who only have a small number of vehicles of having to keep a spare truck and driver on call in case of a breakdown somewhere in their delivery logistics. This may also be an opportunity for them to outsource their entire logistical service to us too.

Tips on using this tool

Focus on combining growth opportunities from the individual elements of the equation to form super-opportunities in the *Excellence in results* at the end. Try to make combinations that haven't been made before.

Tool 15: Beyond the Edge

Exploring the boundaries of where your business relationship with the customers stops and another business takes it over – to examine what opportunities exist there.

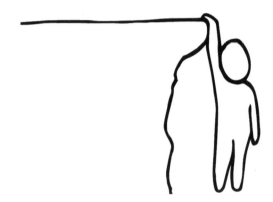

As you are looking for creative ideas that are new for the business, you need to push the issue into new places that potentially haven't been covered before. To achieve this you need to go 'over the edge' and beyond your current realm of business to consider where another business takes over from you in the mind of the customer. Does a gap exist there that can be filled – or created and filled – by you?

How the tool works

This tool looks at where, and how, various aspects of your interaction with a customer stop, and what a possible next step may be for you to take that extends your business domain. This is done by creating a column of current endings in the relationship you have with customers and a second column where each of these can have a 'next step' added. It's these next steps that represent the business opportunities for you. So, start by identifying the product or service that this tool will cover and enter this as your growth focus in the tool.

The paired questions that you now ask are:

What does your product or service do that is the core benefit for the customer?	What does your product or service not do that seems a natural next step in it being used?
If it's a product you sell, what are the related services you offer (if any) that add value to this product?	What value-adding service could you offer that seems a natural extension of this product?
If it's a service you sell, what are the related products you offer (if any) that add value to this product?	What value-adding products could you offer that seem a natural extension of this service?
What well-used features/functions does your product or service currently have?	What are some additional features/functions that you could add and charge more for?
What other companies take over at the edge of where your relationship with the customer ends?	What things do these other companies offer (or do) that could be a part of your proposition?
List some companies who aren't your direct competitors but who are 'nearby' who could potentially do what you do if they wanted to.	What else could they bring to your customers that would be hard for you to compete against? How can you convert this into an opportunity for you?

Here's how two of the current endings of your relationship with a customer appear in the template:

Tool 15: Beyond The Edge

> The growth focus
> for this tool is...

What does your product or service do that is the core benefit for the customer?

What does your product or service <u>not</u> do that seems a natural next step in it being used?

If it's a <u>product</u> you sell, what are the related <u>services</u> you offer (if any) that add value to this product?

What value adding service could you offer that seem a natural extension of this product?

An example of the tool in use

If you work for an online business that sells industrial workwear items, then assume that your growth focus is on the sales of insulated industrial clothing for workers who have to spend a lot of time outdoors in bad weather:

What does your product or service do that is the core benefit for the customer?	What does your product or service not do that seems a natural next step in it being used?
We provide a convenient way for employers to order the clothing their workers need. We help keep the workers warm and dry.	We don't directly help the employee to choose the correct size of item they need – so offer ways to help customers select the correct size. Issue them with a bulk consignment stock where we just review the month-end usage and invoice them accordingly. We aren't helpful in offering layers that the employee can remove if they start to get too hot – find a way to do this.
If it's a product you sell, what are the related services you offer (if any) that add value to this product?	What value-adding service could you offer that seems a natural extension of this product?
The clothing is the product and we sell it online as a convenient service.	Offer a 12-month guaranteed exchange for all items of clothing that don't last at least this long. Offer to supply name stickers that the employee can use to identify their own overall among the many identical others.
If it's a service you sell, what are the related products you offer (if any) that add value to this product?	What value-adding products could you offer that seem a natural extension of this service?
We don't sell any other products beside our clothing items.	Include personal protective equipment such as hard hats and safety glasses. Offer insulated gloves of different types to suit the work being done. This can range from heavy materials lifting gloves with super-grip coatings to delicate gloves where the worker needs to use fine tools.
What well-used features/ functions does your product or service currently have?	What are some additional features/functions that you could add and charge more for?
The items all have an option to be of a hi-visibility colour for safety. We have a reputation for supplying high-quality products.	Include a clip-on emergency whistle to attract co-workers attention when a risk occurs. Offer a guarantee through a no-tear warranty. Free replacements plus another item if our product is at fault.

What other companies take over at the edge of where your relationship with the customer ends?	What things do these other companies offer (or do) that could be a part of your proposition?
Other companies supply the branded labels of our clients' names. Footwear suppliers provide the safety boots. The individuals have to clean their own clothes at home.	Offer to brand our workwear with the client's name or division. Create coloured items of workwear specifically to match a client's brand colours. Offer our own range of footwear – or have a partnership with a footwear supplier. Sell special detergents/cleaning products to get the overalls clean regardless of the level of dirtiness. Partner with an industrial clothing cleaning company to provide a weekly laundering service for the overalls.
List some companies who aren't your direct competitors but who are 'near competitors' who could potentially do what you do if they wanted to.	What else could they bring to your customers that would be hard for you to compete against? How can you convert this into an opportunity for you?
The suppliers of the safety equipment the workers use. Corporate gift suppliers. Thermal underwear/ inner layer suppliers could alleviate the need for our thermal coats.	Provide toggles on our clothing to fasten a specific supplier's equipment to (e.g. a hard hat) so it doesn't get blown off in stormy weather. Sell a complete set of worker's needs so the employer doesn't have to go to multiple suppliers. What ideas can we copy from the unusual items that corporate gift suppliers create for their customers? What if the thermal protection wasn't in the heavy coat outer-layer but was provided by inner-layers and underwear that we could provide? Is there a Velcro-attached chest insulator that can be removed and put in a pocket if the person gets too warm and which eliminates the need for them to take their overalls off to remove a layer?

Tips on using this tool

It's important that in the second column you don't just say the opposite of what's in the first column as this won't add the value you need.

Also, don't try to extend too far beyond your current business activities – you are looking to identify opportunities that can be delivered in the short to medium timeframes. It may feel exciting to be considering big and dramatic opportunities for your business, but these should be saved for another exercise where the focus is on the more strategic and longer-term opportunities.

Assessment and building stage

Review all your ideas and identify the ten that you believe to be the most interesting and beneficial in answering the Killer Question and that can be delivered in the short to medium term. Mark these with the letters 'A' to 'J' in the small boxes in your Genius Spaces. The letters can be written in any order as this isn't a ranking exercise – it's just an identification process. You can now proceed to complete the Boundary Riding summary which is shown below:

Boundary Riding: SUMMARY

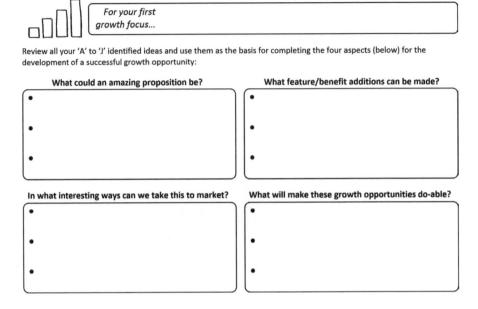

For your first
growth focus...

Review all your 'A' to 'J' identified ideas and use them as the basis for completing the four aspects (below) for the development of a successful growth opportunity:

What could an amazing proposition be?

-
-
-

What feature/benefit additions can be made?

-
-
-

In what interesting ways can we take this to market?

-
-
-

What will make these growth opportunities do-able?

-
-
-

There are five sections in the summary – one for each of your growth focus areas. Copy your first growth focus into the top block and then consider the four aspects posed in the spaces below on the template.

These four aspects cover the specific areas of: creating amazing propositions; additional features and benefits; ways to take the opportunity to the market; and ways to make these suggestions practical and easily do-able. To help you shape your solutions for each growth focus, you should initially consider the 'A' to 'J' ideas that you've identified, as these are the ones you regard as the best. However, review all your other ideas too, for they can also add value in creating a great opportunity. If you feel that your 'A' to 'J' ideas should feature in more than one growth focus – then that's fine. What matters is the potential for success – *regardless of where the idea components come from.*

Some of the ideas that you've identified may excite you – but you recognise that these are impossible to deliver in the required timeframe. It's important not to lose these, so review your ideas again and identify *two* that will require a significant amount of time and/or resources to deliver, but which will potentially have a massive impact on growing this part of your business. Mark these two ideas with a star in the idea's small box and then copy them into the space at the end of the Boundary Riding summary section – shown below:

Boundary Riding: SUMMARY

Your two longer-term opportunities:

Longer-term idea #1	Longer-term idea #2

You'll notice how each of these five tools has focused on the generic Killer Question of growing revenues through ideas that can be delivered in relatively short timeframes. Naturally, some of the ideas you'll have identified will be much bigger in scale and require a longer timeframe to develop and execute. These ideas won't be lost as they will remain in your completed template – as long as you keep it somewhere safe.

These questions and considerations of growth that you've asked and answered, will be enduring in nature as your organisation will always need growth. So those ideas that you haven't highlighted as being among your best to take forward may potentially be useful in the future.

Your Boundary Riding project is now complete and you can take your best ideas forward and shape them into your winning ideas as discussed previously.

Using The Idea Generator in teams

When you've achieved success as The Idea Generator on your own, you may want to run another exercise with a team of people. In previous chapters you read about getting people to buy in to your Killer Question when you start, and also how you present your winning ideas to get them on-board with the solution and execution. Well, there's a way to get them involved throughout, by you leading a thinking project where all participants act as The Idea Generator.

You now know the serious drawbacks with brainstorming workshops where people try to think as a group to identify new ideas. With The Idea Generator, the people you invite to be part of your project team think as individuals, at the times when it's best for them, and then come together in a workshop to synergise their outputs as a team. This concluding workshop is called a Synergising Session and brings the participants together to share their best ideas and to collaborate in creating the optimum solutions that will deliver greatest value and success in answer to the Killer Question.

There are three stages to running The Idea Generator team project:

1 Setting up your project
2 Allocating a thinking focus to the participants
3 Running your Synergising Session

Let's look at each of these stages in detail.

1. Setting up your project

You need to download The Idea Generator leader's guide from the same internet location as the toolset templates: **www.TheIdeaGenerator. info**

This Microsoft Word document is free to download and guides you through setting up and customising The Idea Generator project to suit your needs.

The first activity is to create your Killer Question which was covered in Chapter 3, and the setting up of a Killer Question is the same process whether an individual is going to answer it or a team. Once the Killer Question is finalised, identify which toolset is most appropriate for it and modify your leader's guide to suit this. Note that there is only one leader's guide which contains instructions for all three toolsets. You simply delete the two sections which aren't relevant to your needs.

Next you have to identify the participants who will be part of your thinking project team. Naturally, you'll need to involve some of the key stakeholders, but you may also want to involve people from different parts of the business who can give you fresh and relevant perspectives. You may even consider people from outside of your organisation such as suppliers, customers or delivery partners. The ideal number to be involved is between five and ten people, including you.

2. Allocating a thinking focus to the participants

For the Islands of Opportunity toolset, all participants use the five tools on the same Killer Question in order to achieve the widest range of perspectives for your Killer Question.

With the Divide and Conquer toolset, the leader (you) needs to set up the tool and identify the exhausted areas and then to establish the challenging areas that you want your team to work on. To get the most benefit from this toolset you can allocate a different challenging area for individual people to use with specific tools. A matrix-style allocation tool is included in the leader's guide for this purpose.

The Boundary Riding toolset requires you to allocate specific growth focus areas to each tool. Tool 12 (Four Customer Lenses) requires the use of a customer persona – and you as the leader can determine which of your established company personas should be used. If you don't have any existing customer personas, then you can specify the type that each participant should create to represent a specific current or non-current customer segment.

For Islands of Opportunity the thinking focus is solely the Killer Question. However, with the other toolsets the benefit of allocating a more prescriptive thinking focus is that you can begin to zoom in on specific aspects of the Killer Question to enable a deeper level of interrogation to be achieved than would happen without an allocated focus area. This allocation feature gives the leader the flexibility to assign specific areas to specific people where appropriate, to get the most effective use from the knowledge and capabilities of the individual participants. It can sometimes be preferable to allocate people to different areas than those they would naturally be expected to handle – again to enhance the value of fresh perspectives delivering new insights.

When your leader's guide is completed, you then send each of the participants a digital copy. It includes instructions on how they download their template and the timeframes for your thinking project. Five to seven working days should be sufficient for the participants to complete a template on most projects. You will also need to invite the participants to a Synergising Session which occurs at the end of your project's thinking period.

3. Running your Synergising Session

The preferred option is to invite the participants to a Synergising Session at which you lead a guided process where their best ideas are assimilated and synergised to produce a valuable and compelling answer to the Killer Question posed. The Synergising Session enables people to arrive with their thinking already done, so they can spend the workshop time more effectively in identifying how the value of the selected ideas will be achieved and delivered.

The Synergising Sessions are run differently depending on which of the toolsets your team has used and are described individually below. The leader's guide contains a checklist of materials needed and things to prepare for the Synergising Session, as well as a run-sheet to help you manage the session.

Islands of Opportunity Synergising Session

The first activity is to write up the Killer Question on a flipchart sheet and stick it on the wall as a continual reminder to the participants of what the focus of the thinking project was – and still is.

Then get each person in the session to write a brief summary of their top four ideas, each on a separate sticky-note. Go around the table asking each person to briefly explain their #4-ranked idea and put these up on a flipchart. After each person has explained their idea, go around the table again asking people for interesting combinations or connections they can make that will boost the ideas presented. Capture all useful comments on sticky-notes.

Then repeat the cycle with each person's #3-ranked idea and add all these onto the flipchart. When ways to boost these ideas are asked for, they can include any of the previously stated #4 ideas already on the flipchart. Repeat the cycle again for the #2-ranked ideas, and finally the #1-ranked ideas.

When all the ideas are up on flipcharts, as a group you can move the sticky-notes around to assemble the ideas into themes, solutions or opportunities. Aim to compile interesting combinations of ideas that form discrete solutions to the Killer Question. As soon as the solution looks reasonably well-formed, stick these onto a sheet of A3 paper and give it a title that summarises the theme. Then move on to create another compilation of ideas on another A3 sheet. Avoid adding too many ideas such that one theme becomes the epic, all-encompassing showcase of everything delightful. If this starts to happen, break this theme down into smaller components and keep them separated. Sometimes you may have to copy an idea onto another sticky-note as it needs to be on two or more A3 sheets at the same time. Some of these solution-themes may only contain two to four sticky-notes while others may have five to eight on.

When there seems to be no more compilations to be made, consider what's left on the flipchart. Some of the sticky-notes may be duplicates and can be disposed of – but watch out for the ones which aren't exact duplicates, for there may be value in the way that they are subtly different from the ones to which they are similar. Of the non-duplicate sticky-notes that are left, assess whether there is anything that could form an interesting solution-theme to the Killer Question and if so create another named A3 sheet.

At the end, review the various themes that have been created and ask for any final comments or suggestions on how to boost these further.

Divide and Conquer Synergising Session

The format is similar in style to the Islands of Opportunity process, but each of the CHALLENGING areas is discussed in turn. The first activity is to write the Killer Question on a flipchart sheet and stick it on the wall to ensure the participants remain focused on the goal of the thinking project.

Entitle a flipchart sheet with the first CHALLENGING area 'A' and ask the participants to review their outputs for this CHALLENGING area and to create three sticky-notes, one for each of their top three ideas that capture what they believe to be their most interesting ways to address it. Then go around the table asking people in turn to briefly state their ideas, and stick them on the flipchart sheet as they are read out.

Once everyone has given their feedback, stimulate a discussion on how these could be integrated, connected and developed to add value for the business in some way. Note down all relevant comments and ensure that any additional ideas are captured on individual sticky-notes and added to the flipchart sheet. Only allow five minutes for this discussion and ask people to be concise and brief in their comments. (The run-sheet in the leader's guide will assist you with your timings when you run your session.)

Then move on to the second CHALLENGING area and repeat the process using a new flipchart sheet. Continue in this manner until all five CHALLENGING areas have been reviewed. At the end of the process you will have five sheets around the walls, one for each of the CHALLENGING areas.

The final stage of the Synergising Session is to re-focus the team on the Killer Question and to review the outputs on all the flipchart sheets to create an action list of possible activities for moving the opportunities forward.

Boundary Riding Synergising Session

There are only three areas to consider – one for each of the five growth focus areas. Start by writing your Killer Question on a flipchart sheet and stick it on the wall to focus the team on the goal of the thinking project.

Title five flipchart sheets each with the name of one of the five growth focus areas you used in the project and divide each sheet into four quadrants with the headings as shown below.

Growth focus #1

Amazing proposition	Features / benefits
Take to market	Make it do-able

These areas will lead the collation and development of the best ideas as follows:

- **Amazing proposition:** What could we do that would make this product/service appear to be an amazing proposition in the eyes of the customer?
- **Feature/benefits:** What opportunities exist to enhance the features and customer benefits of this product/service?
- **Take to market:** What interesting routes are there to get this product/service into the market and in front of potential customers?
- **Make it do-able:** What ways are there to make these suggestions practical and readily implementable in the business to ensure we achieve the growth we are looking for?

For the first product/service focus, allow people ten minutes to write their three suggestions they have for each quadrant area. They should already have done this in their template and so will just be copying them onto sticky-notes. However, there is another purpose in getting them to rewrite their ideas. They probably completed the template at least a day ago (if not longer) and in that time the Killer Question and the ideas they generated will have been percolating in their subconscious minds. When they rewrite their idea in your Synthesising Session, they may well amend it slightly for the better based on other thoughts that have occurred to them in the mean-time. When writing their ideas down, they should only write one idea per sticky-note.

Start with the first focus area and ask each person to read out their three ideas for the first quadrant in turn and stick these onto the flip-chart. Once all the ideas are up, proceed with the second quadrant and then the third and fourth quadrants in turn.

When all feedback has been given, stimulate a discussion on what courses of action could be taken to ensure success in growing this opportunity. Consider what hurdles may need to be overcome and what other people or activities need to be included to help boost the potential for success of this opportunity. Capture all these comments and add them onto the flipchart. When this growth focus has been concluded, repeat the same process for the remaining four growth focus areas.

Closing out your Synergising Session

Go around the room and ask each person what their individual recommendations are to deliver the optimum value for all the items discussed in the Synergising Session. You should make notes on the key comments made by each person. This approach is preferable to either voting on the best ideas or asking the whole group what to do, as you can later review the individual recommendations to determine your own course of action to take.

This may seem a counter-intuitive thing to do, but in the light of a new day, once all the ideas have assimilated themselves inside your subconscious, the decisions made in the spur of the moment during the Synergising Session may not always be the best course of action to take. If you go counter to a decision made by a group in a meeting, that can tend to exclude people by the manner in which you arbitrarily change the group's decision. However, if you make it clear at the conclusion of the Synergising Session that you will take all their recommendations away and review them thoroughly afterwards – before determining a course of action – this will seem reasonable.

Nothing stops you from shaping one or more considered courses of action after the Synergising Session and then asking for their feedback as to which to take – but as you've developed each one of the options, you will probably be comfortable with progressing any of them.

Another action to take in the meeting is to ask if there are any other programmes or projects occurring in the business that the range of solutions or opportunities on the flipcharts will benefit from, or can support. Additionally, it's good to be aware of programmes or projects that the ideas may run contrary to, or which will end up duplicating something else which already has a head-start in the business. These are all things that can help you review and make a more considered decision about your next steps going forward after the session rather than in the session.

As you develop your preferred approach to answering the Killer Question under consideration, refer back to the section on shaping winning ideas. While some senior managers might want a finalised plan that they can simply sign off, others may want to put some input into the solution. So enable this – let your ideas act as offers to invite them to be involved, and leave some elements open or with a range of options for their input. You will have developed some new and potentially innovative ways forward running The Idea Generator – so encourage the senior management to be involved in the final shaping of the solution. After all, this is the key to winning ideas.

An alternative to running a Synergising Session

With a conventional brainstorming session, it's necessary to have all the participants attend a meeting at a common venue – which can be expensive in time and cost if people have to travel any distance. With The Idea Generator approach, people from around the globe can download and complete the template under your guidance as the leader – which is a great way to involve people who may not always be included due to their location or situation regarding working times and/or days.

The alternative to running a Synergising Session is for you to meet with some or all of the participants individually to go through each of their outputs either face-to-face or via a phone call or video call. You can then collate their outputs yourself to incorporate into potential solutions. Also, you can run a hybrid approach where you speak with the individuals who cannot attend your Synergising Session before the event and you input their information on their behalf to the others who do attend. The Idea Generator process can flex to suit your needs under any situation.

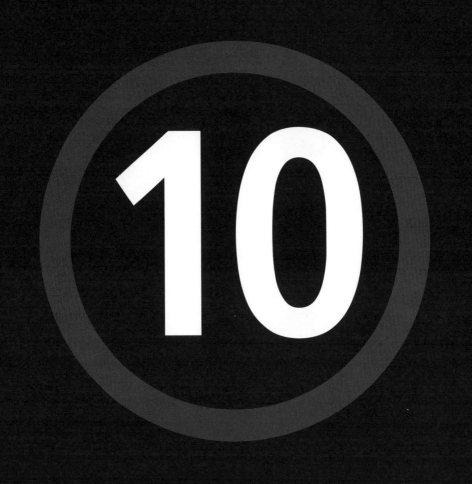

Unleashing the corporate creativity

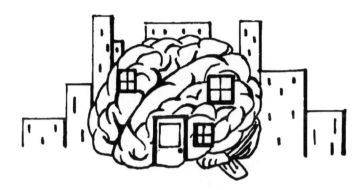

Having idea schemes in businesses seems intuitively to make sense. Establish a simple mechanism whereby employees can submit ideas that will benefit the business, and usually with some kind of reward or merit scheme for those ideas which are implemented. Unfortunately, very few idea schemes have been successful and many companies no longer run them – which may seem peculiar for something which appears to make good business sense.

You've seen the importance of asking Killer Questions that are of value to the business, however, the problem with idea schemes is this – the ideas submitted are answers to questions that aren't being asked. Even if the idea is a brilliant answer to a question, if that question isn't on any senior manager's agenda, then they aren't going to be interested in taking action to execute it. This becomes demoralising for staff, as their great ideas – and in the overview of things they are of value – just aren't being implemented. As one of the criteria for the success of an idea scheme is that around 25–33 per cent of the ideas should be implemented, and as this doesn't happen, this becomes the root cause of the ultimate demise of the scheme.

So what other things can be done that will create and deliver significant value for the business?

The Cascaded Question

How do you get an entire organisation to answer one question that they know is of value to them? The answer is simple. You just need to ask the question!

As an example of a Killer Question that would be valid for most businesses and organisations, here's one focused around growth:

How can we achieve an additional 5 per cent revenue growth over and above the targets we have planned for the next 12 months?

The key word in this Killer Question is *achieve* because this aligns the question to the fact that the growth needs to be delivered within the defined period. This helps to contain the thinking output to ideas that can be developed and executed quickly in order to deliver the value within the timeframe. This stops the ideas from being too far from the way the business works at the moment. This is controlled thinking around natural extensions of what is currently done in the business and is termed organic growth. Anything too different would require bigger, time-consuming changes which would prevent the value from being achieved within the specified timeframe.

If this Killer Question were posed by the executive team, it would cascade down to the next level to use The Idea Generator to identify what the high-level opportunities could be. Should this additional 5 per cent come from one specific area or customer segment, or should it be spread across numerous areas – or every area of the business? The cascaded Killer Question for this next tier of management may then be:

What opportunities does [our area] have to develop additional 5 per cent revenues this year?

When numerous specific areas have been identified, for example specific product areas, then each of those product areas can ask their own cascaded version of the Killer Question, which may be formed as:

How can we extend the XYZ product into new markets this year to gain 5 per cent growth?

The functional areas that support the product areas also need to ask their own Killer Questions that will assist in the successful growth of the product areas. The marketing department's Killer Question could be:

What innovative and low-cost marketing initiatives could be used to help stimulate demand for our XYZ product from the category 3 and category 4 market segments this year?

While the servicing department Killer Question might be:

How can our service engineers encourage customers to upgrade from the older ABC product to the newer XYZ product that we want to grow this year?

When it comes to setting the cascaded questioning approach, the departments who are involved higher up, and so earlier in the process, can identify the Killer Questions that they would like to have answered by all the support areas they interact with – and challenge these areas to answer them. This can actually help the support areas, who may not have known the best question to ask, and who will appreciate the valuable input.

In this manner the executive-level Killer Question can cascade throughout the organisation to ensure everyone is involved with a challenging thinking exercise and is part of the overall team helping to identify the additional business growth – which will benefit all concerned.

Finding a brilliant Killer Question

In some organisations there's a culture of not sticking your neck out for fear of getting your head sliced off. An example might be that if an exciting and opportune new idea was proposed by a senior manager, they would be told to get it done – but without any additional resources or change to their objectives for the year. This kind of environment stymies the suggesting of new ideas this way.

An alternative approach would be for the CEO to issue a challenge to the business for all senior managers to propose the Killer Question that they believe would add most value in a given timeframe for the business. They don't have to provide the answers at this stage – just the Killer Question itself. All these Killer Questions can be reviewed and the one (or more) that is deemed to show the most potential can be supported with resources and a budget to make it a success. This can be a showcase project such that when it is deemed to be delivering great value, then more Killer Questions can be allocated an execution budget – or another call for new Killer Questions can be issued across the business.

An interesting extension is that the competition could be widened to include all employees and not just senior managers. It was stated how idea schemes tend to fail because the ideas are answers to questions that weren't being asked – but what if you put in place a Killer Question scheme where people submit the questions they believe should be asked – and not the answers?

Again, as an alternative to an idea scheme, once a cascaded Killer Questioning process is established within an organisation, then an idea scheme in the form of an answer scheme – where people could submit their answers to the various Killer Questions being asked – could be set up. This naturally would overcome the key issue with failed idea schemes in that every idea is an answer to a question that is openly and actively being asked within the business.

Having a stock of Killer Questions

As another approach, what if it was part of every manager's role to identify three Killer Questions for their area every year. It's a fact of business that the people lower down the corporate pyramid are closer to the customer than those at the top, while those at the top are more attuned to the strategic direction of the industry and economy. Where different levels of management meet, they can each propose a Killer Question and then discuss which is most likely to deliver the greater value in relation to the ease with which it can be implemented. A battle of the Killer Questions if you like. While these growth questions can be cascaded down as suggested previously, they can also float up to find the most senior sponsor who recognises it as a great question for the business to ask.

With each manager having their three Killer Questions identified, if any of their line employees came to them asking for a Killer Question that they could address, they would immediately have one they could provide to match the employee's zeal. Remember, this employee could easily be you – when you ask your manager for a Killer Question on which The Idea Generator can be applied.

A final challenge for you . . .

Killer Questions don't have to be posed by the executive. Anyone can pose one for themselves. If you've got a team working for you, then why not identify the question that will be good for you to pose – and for you and your team to subsequently answer? Just make sure you follow the guidelines for posing a great Killer Question to maximise your potential for success.

Here's one last challenge for you – but one with a difference. All you have to do is either have a brief meeting, make a phone call, or send an email, where you ask an appropriate member of your executive team 'What's the Killer Question that our business/organisation needs to answer in the coming year?' Explain how you'd like to use a new approach to identify answers to this question.

Whatever Killer Question your business cares to pose shouldn't worry you at all now. Why? Because you've become The Idea Generator – and are capable of answering any question that's put to you!

What did you think of this book?

We're really keen to hear from you about this book, so that we can make our publishing even better.

Please log on to the following website and leave us your feedback.

It will only take a few minutes and your thoughts are invaluable to us.

www.pearsoned.co.uk/bookfeedback

Index

strong focus 42–3
structured approach 37–9
time and space for thinking 40–2
modifying existing ideas 60–7,
    98–104
motivation 42–3

NASA research on creativity 16–17
neurons 44–5
new thinking projects
    Killer Question examples 33
    toolset for see Islands of
        Opportunity toolset
notebooks 50

old problems
    Killer Question examples 34
    toolset for see Divide and Conquer
        toolset
organic growth see growth
    opportunities
other industries, perspectives of
    98–104
other people
    avoiding interruptions from 41–2,
        43, 44
    involving in your thinking 46

pen and paper vs. technology 49–50
personal perspectives (alter ego)
    108–12
personas, customer 128–34
perspectives
    customers 128–34
    other industries 98–104
    personal (alter ego) 108–12
    unconventional 56–9
presenting your ideas 88–9, 163–4
problem areas
    Killer Question examples 34
    toolset for see Divide and Conquer
        toolset
project approach to thinking 38
project categories 33–5

quality vs. quantity 19, 74
Querencia 28–9
questions
    fear of 13–14, 28
    interrogating your 30–3
    see also Killer Questions
Quirky Equation tool 140–6

Rapid Thinking tool 67–74
re-phrasing tool 105–8
research on creativity 16–18
rituals 44
Robinson, Sir Ken 10

Sawyer, Keith 18
self-motivation 42–3
'So what?' test 32
solutions, looking for 14
stealing existing ideas 60–7, 98–104
subconscious thinking 45–6, 117,
    162, 163
Synergising Sessions 158–64

teams 51, 155–64
    allocating thinking focuses 156–7
    challenging the consensus 21–2
    setting up the project 156
    synergising session alternative
        164
    synergising sessions 158–64
templates 50–1, 52
terminology 51–2
thinking
    attitude to 43–4
    a new way for business 25–6
    out-thinking yourself 39–40
    outdated 9–23
    'outside the box' 38
    structured approach 37–9
    subconscious 45–6, 117, 162, 163
    time for 17, 20, 40–2
    what you know vs. what you don't
        know 28
Three-Word Sentence tool 105–8

time
  demands on 15–16
  for thinking 17, 20, 40–2
tools and toolsets
  choosing 52–3
  definitions 51–2
  Genius Spaces 53
  pen and paper *vs.* technology
    49–50
  templates 50–1
  see also Boundary Riding toolset;
    Divide and Conquer toolset;
    Islands of Opportunity toolset

Unconventional Perspectives tool
  56–9

viewpoints *see* perspectives
voting on ideas 22

winning ideas 26–7

Zuckerberg, Mark 29–30